A Student's Companion to Hacker Handbooks

Contributing Authors

Sylvia Basile
Midlands Technical College

Sandra Chumchal
Blinn College

Sarah Gottschall
Prince George's Community College

Paul Madachy
Prince George's Community College

 **bedford/st.martin's**
Macmillan Learning
Boston | New York

For information, write: Bedford/St. Martin's, 75 Arlington Street, Boston, MA 02116

ISBN 978-1-319-21274-2

Acknowledgments

James J. Bernstein and Joseph Bernstein, "Texting at the Light and Other Forms of Device Distraction behind the Wheel," *BMC Public Health* 15 (2015), 968; doi: 10.1186/s12889-015-2343-8. (Accessed from https://www.ncbi.nlm.nih.gov/pmc/articles/PMC4584002.) Copyright © 2015 James J. Bernstein and Joseph Bernstein. This article is distributed under the terms of the Creative Commons Attribution 4.0 International License: http://creativecommons.org/licenses/by/4.0/.

Debra Kahn, "Melting Ice Could Cause More California Droughts," *E&E News*, December 5, 2017, https://www.eenews.net/stories/1060068087/. Copyright © 2017. Reprinted by permission.

A Note for Instructors

The information, activities, tools, and exercises in this workbook offer developing college writers help with and practice in key writing, research, and grammar skills. *A Student's Companion to Hacker Handbooks* can be used to give students in paired, co-requisite, or "ALP" sections of composition success-building extra practice with a variety of topics. The exercises in the workbook can be used in a variety of ways:

✧ homework

✧ classroom practice

✧ quizzes

✧ individualized self-teaching assignments

✧ writing center or learning lab worksheets

If you have adopted a Hacker/Sommers handbook for your course, you may want to consult the chart on the inside back cover, which correlates the content in this workbook with the coverage in the handbooks—*Rules for Writers*, *A Writer's Reference*, *A Pocket Style Manual*, *The Bedford Handbook*, and *Writer's Help*.

The workbook is organized in four parts. **Part 1** covers the transition from high school writing to college writing and includes important strategies for college success, such as managing your time and using academic etiquette. **Part 2** discusses topics common to first-year composition courses: essay and paragraph development, active reading, audience awareness, peer review, revision, and working with sources. Each of the chapters includes brief reflective activities. **Part 3** contains exercises in a variety of rhetorical and research skills, such as using topic sentences, avoiding plagiarism, and reading critically. **Part 4** includes exercises in sentence-level topics: parallelism, subject-verb agreement, avoiding fragments, using commas and quotation marks, and more.

Exercises and activities are spaced so that students can complete their work in this workbook. Answers for most of the exercises in Parts 3 and 4 are included in the back of this book for convenience.

This workbook is available for student purchase—in print and digital options.

- ❖ *A Student's Companion to Hacker Handbooks* (stand-alone): ISBN 978-1-319-21274-2.
- ❖ *A Student's Companion to Hacker Handbooks* packaged with a Hacker/Sommers handbook, available at a significant discount:

A Student's Companion to Hacker Handbooks packaged with	Use ISBN
Rules for Writers, Ninth Edition	978-1-319-22752-4
Rules for Writers with Writing about Literature, Ninth Edition	978-1-319-22754-8
A Writer's Reference, Ninth Edition	978-1-319-24248-0
A Writer's Reference with Exercises, Ninth Edition	978-1-319-24250-3
A Writer's Reference with Writing about Literature, Ninth Edition	978-1-319-24252-7
A Pocket Style Manual, Eighth Edition	978-1-319-24251-0
The Bedford Handbook, Tenth Edition	978-1-319-24249-7

- ❖ LaunchPad Solo for Hacker Handbooks, LaunchPad for *A Writer's Reference*, and Writer's Help 2.0 will all include *A Student's Companion to Hacker Handbooks* for Fall 2019 classes.
- ❖ *A Student's Companion to Hacker Handbooks* is also available in a variety of e-book formats. Visit **macmillanlearning.com/ebooks** to learn more.

And of course we at Bedford/St. Martin's are available for you—whether you are new to our print and media products, new to this course, or in need of new ideas. Contact your sales representative to find out how we can help.

Contents

PART 4 *Practicing Sentence-Level Skills* 175

CHAPTER 1

Becoming a college writer

Think for a minute about your high school writing experiences—perhaps you wrote an analysis of *The Adventures of Huckleberry Finn*, one or more lab reports for biology, a response to a film about Afghanistan, and a poem about growing up. You may find that when you get to college, more writing is expected, but also more is expected of you as a writer. Sometimes you'll wonder why no one is telling you what the "more" is or exactly how college writing differs from high school writing.

What's certain is that you will be required to write in almost all of your college courses—even if you major in engineering, nursing, or business. Developing different attitudes toward and approaches to academic writing can help you to become a successful writer in all of your college courses.

✦ **1a** Be open minded about the "rules" of good writing

Think for a moment about all the rules of good writing that you learned throughout elementary, middle, and high school. Which rules have really stuck in your mind? Which ones do you follow without question?

WRITING ACTIVITY ✦ Take a few minutes to write down four or five rules about writing that you learned in your past school experiences. Did you find these rules useful? Paralyzing? Confusing? Clear?

✎
_____

_____

_____

_____

_____

The five-paragraph essay. In the previous writing activity, you may have talked about the five-paragraph essay, a form of writing taught in many middle schools and high schools in the United States. It requires an introduction, three body paragraphs, and a conclusion. It was probably a useful formula for you as you composed in-class essays and essays for standardized tests. But the kind of writing you will be asked to do in college may be too complex and require too much analysis for the form to continue to work for you. Be open to writing longer essays and using different types of organization. Be open to composing a hybrid of paragraphs and visuals. Be open to writing that is not restricted to reporting information or giving a personal response; many college assignments ask you to combine those purposes with other purposes, such as analyzing and arguing.

Using first person ("I" or "we"). A lot of high school writing is awkward to read because of rules related to the point of view of an essay. In college, you will need to learn about your professors' expectations, but be open to the idea that for some writing the use of "I" and "we" may in fact be encouraged. College professors may expect you to write with a more personal voice, rather than using stale sentences such as "One might argue that one has the right to free speech in social media posts. . . ." You may also be expected to report field research experiences or steps in other research with "I" or "we." You will find that some college professors have strong feelings about this topic, so asking before a draft is due is a good idea.

Collaborating with other writers and thinkers. You may have had an experience in which a teacher questioned a written response that sounded too much like a classmate's or specifically prohibited working on writing assignments with others in the class. College professors in a first-year course expect you to do your own writing and to cite sources when you borrow language or ideas from another writer, but they also want to prepare you for courses and workplace tasks in which collaboration will be expected. You will find that college assignments often require collaboration and encourage you to seek feedback. Teachers will expect you to approach academic writing tasks as a participant in a world of ideas rather than as a reporter of others' ideas. You can think of research writing as collaborating, in a sense, with other thinkers in order to answer a research question. You will be expected to cite published sources, of course, but casual conversations you have with classmates, writing center staff, peers, and others can inform your thinking about a subject you will write about.

✦ 1b Adopt good habits of mind

College writing gives you the opportunity to develop skills, such as supporting arguments with evidence, writing effective thesis statements, and using transitions well, but it also gives you the opportunity to develop habits. Successful college students develop certain "habits of mind," a way of approaching learning that leads to success.

In 2011, the Council of Writing Program Administrators (CWPA), the National Council of Teachers of English (NCTE), and the National Writing Project (NWP) identified eight habits of mind that successful college students adopt. The following overview is adapted from the three organizations' report "Framework for Success in Postsecondary Writing."

Curiosity. Are you the kind of person who always wants to know more? This habit of mind will serve you well in courses in which your curiosity about issues, problems, people, or policies can form the backbone of a writing project.

WRITING ACTIVITY ✦ What are you most curious to learn about? What experiences have you had in which your curiosity has led you to an interesting discovery or to more questions?

_____

_____

_____

_____

Openness. Some people are more open than others to new ideas and experiences and new ways of thinking about the world. Being open to other perspectives and positions can help you to frame sound arguments and counterarguments and solve other college writing challenges in thoughtful ways.

WRITING ACTIVITY ✦ In the family or part of the world in which you grew up, did people tend to be very open, not open at all, or somewhere in the middle? Thinking about your own level of open-mindedness, reflect on how much or how little your own attitude toward a quality like openness is a result of the attitudes of the people around you.

_____

_____

_____

_____

Engagement. Successful college writers are involved in their own learning process. Students who are engaged put effort into their classes, knowing that they'll get something out of their classes—something other than a grade. They participate in their own learning by planning, seeking feedback when they need to, and communicating with peers and professors to create their own success.

WRITING ACTIVITY ✦ Write about a few of the ways you try (or plan to try) to be involved in your own learning. What does "engagement" look like for you?

_____

_____

_____

_____

Creativity. You may be thinking that you have to be an artist, poet, or musician to display creativity. Not so. Scientists use creativity every day in coming up with ways to investigate questions in their field. Engineers and technicians approach problem solving in creative ways. Retail managers use creativity in displaying merchandise and motivating employees.

WRITING ACTIVITY ✦ Think about the field you plan to enter. What forms might "creativity" take in that field?

_____

_____

_____

_____

Persistence. You are probably used to juggling long-term and short-term commitments—both in school and in your everyday life. Paying attention to your commitments and being persistent enough to see them through, even when the commitments are challenging, are good indicators that you will be successful in college.

WRITING ACTIVITY ✦ Describe a time when you faced and overcame an obstacle in an academic setting. What did you learn from that experience?

_____

_____

_____

_____

Responsibility. College will require you to be responsible in ways you may not have had to be before. Two responsibilities you will face as an academic writer are to represent the ideas of others fairly and to give credit to writers whose ideas and language you borrow for your own purposes.

WRITING ACTIVITY ✦ Why do you think academic responsibility is important? What kind of experience have you had already with this kind of responsibility?

_____

_____

_____

_____

Flexibility. Would your friends say that you are the kind of person who can just "go with the flow"? Do you adapt easily to changing situations? If so, you will find college easier, especially college writing. When you find, for example, that you've written a draft that doesn't address the right audience or that your peer review group doesn't understand at all, you will be able to adapt. Being flexible enough to adapt to the demands of different writing projects is an important habit of mind.

WRITING ACTIVITY ✦ Describe a situation in which you've had to make changes based on a situation you couldn't control. Did you do so easily or with difficulty?

_____

_____

_____

_____

Metacognition (reflection). As a learner, you have probably been asked to think back on a learning experience and comment on what went well or not well, what you learned or wish you had learned, or what decisions you made or didn't make. Writers who reflect on their own processes and decisions are better able to transfer writing skills to future assignments.

WRITING ACTIVITY ✦ Reflect on your many experiences as a writer. What was your most satisfying experience as a writer? What made it so?

_____

_____

_____

_____

_____

_____

_____

_____

_____

CHAPTER 2

Time management

You might be the kind of student who is content to spend hours making flashcards and outlining your notes in different colored ink. Or maybe you're good at channeling your adrenaline, often starting a twenty-page term paper the night before it's due.

The problem is that both of these approaches carry risk. Goof off and you may fail all your courses. Do nothing but stare at your laptop in the library for weeks on end and you'll wind up dull, pasty, and miserable. If you're like most of us, you'll learn more, get better grades, and have more fun in college if you operate somewhere in the middle.

By now, you've probably heard the Latin expression *carpe diem*, which translates to "seize the day" (as in, make time work for you). Mastering the art of time management is one key to your future success and happiness, but learning to make time work for you can be a challenge.

✦ 2a The case for time management

Why bother? We know. Some students don't want to "waste" time on planning and managing their schedules. Instead, they prefer to go with the flow. Unfortunately, the demands of college (not to mention most careers) require serious, intentional strategies. Unless you can afford to hire a personal assistant, any "slacker habits" you may have relied on in the past won't carry you through.

To psych yourself up, think of time management as part of your life skill set. If you're trying to remember all the things you need to get done, it's hard to focus on actually doing the work. Organizing your time well accomplishes three things. First, it optimizes your chances of getting good results by ensuring that you're not flying by the seat of your pants. Second, it enhances your life by saving you from stress and regret. And finally, it reflects what you value. It's all about doing your best.

Remember that people who learn good time management techniques in college generally soar in their careers. If you're more efficient at your job, you'll be able to accomplish more. That will lend you a competitive advantage over your coworkers. Your bosses will learn to depend on you, and they may reward you with interesting projects, promotions, and educational and training opportunities. You'll feel empowered and positive—and may even have more time for a social life, which has been shown to lower stress and advance careers.

✦ 2b Taking charge of your time

Freedom can be a dangerous thing. One of the biggest differences between high school and college is that you find yourself with far more independence—and greater responsibility—than you've ever known. If you are continuing your education after a break, you may be contending with family or work obligations, too. But it would be a mistake to assume that Oprah, rocket scientists, and other type-A folks have some kind of monopoly on organization and focus. You, the ordinary student, can also embrace your inner executive assistant—the one who keeps you on time, on task, and ready for a slice of the action. So how do you begin?

Set some goals. Goals help you figure out where to devote the majority of your time. To achieve your goals, you need to do more than just think about them. You need to act. This requires setting both short-term and long-term goals. When you are determining your long-term goals, it is important to be honest and realistic with yourself. Goals should be challenging, but they should also be attainable. Be sure they align with your abilities, values, and interests. Do you want to go on to further schooling? Have you decided what career you want to pursue? Mulling over these questions can help you start thinking about where you want to be in the next five to ten years. Dreaming up long-term goals can be exciting and fun; however, reaching your goals requires undertaking a number of steps in the short term.

Try to be very specific when determining your short-term goals. For example, if you're committed to becoming an expert in a certain field, you'll want to commit yourself to every class and internship that can help you on your way. A specific goal would be to review your school's course catalog, identify the courses you want to take, and determine when you must take them. An even more specific goal would be to research interesting internship opportunities in your field of study. The good news about goals is that all the small steps add up.

Identify five short-term goals—goals you believe you can accomplish in the next six to twelve months.

1. _____

2. _____

3. _____

4. _____

5. _____

Identify one long-term goal—one that you'd like to accomplish in the next several years.

_____

_____

Now identify three steps that will move you toward your long-term goal.

1. _____

2. _____

3. _____

Know your priorities. To achieve your goals, set your life priorities so that you're steadily working toward them.

◇ **Start out with a winner's mentality.** Make sure your studies take precedence. Having worked so hard to get to college, you cannot allow other activities and *Modern Family* reruns to derail your schoolwork. Review your current commitments and prepare to sacrifice a few—for now. Whatever you do, talk to your family, your boss, and your friends about your college workload and goals so that everyone's on the same page. When you have a looming deadline, be firm. Emphasize that no amount of badgering will succeed in getting you to go to the *Walking Dead* theme party during finals week.

◇ **Next, start preparing for your future.** Visit your campus career center and schedule an assessment test to hone in on your talents and interests. Or, if you know what career you want to pursue, talk with a professional in that field, your guidance counselor, a professor, or an upper-class student in your chosen major to find out what steps you need to take to get the results you want, starting now. What skills and experiences should be on your résumé when you graduate that will make you stand out from the pack? Make a plan, prioritize your goals, and then make a time management schedule.

✧ **Balance is key.** Being realistic about your future and goals may mean making big sacrifices. Be realistic about the present, too. Always include time in your schedule for people who are important to you and time on your own to recharge.

Tip | **Share your Google or Outlook calendar.** *Keeping an electronic copy of your calendar allows you to share it with others at a click of a button. Letting your family, friends, and employer know what is on your plate at any given moment can prevent misunderstandings from arising because of your school commitments and create a more supportive home and work environment.*

Embrace the 2-for-1 rule.
For every hour you spend in class at college, you should plan to study two hours outside of class. That's the standard; so keep it in mind when you're planning your schedule. The bottom line is that you carry more responsibility for your education in college than you did in high school.

Own your class schedule.
Your schedule will affect almost every aspect of your college life. Before you register, think about how to make your schedule work for you.

✧ **Start with your biorhythms.** Do you study more effectively in the day or the evening or a combination of both? Ideally, you should devote your peak hours—when you're most alert and engaged—to schoolwork. Schedule other activities, like doing laundry, emailing, exercising, and socializing, for times when it's harder to concentrate. Start by filling out the chart on page 11.

✧ **If you live on campus,** you might want to create a schedule that situates you near a dining hall at mealtimes or lets you spend breaks between classes at the library. Feel free to slot breaks for relaxation and catching up with friends. But beware of the midday nap. If the nap is longer than thirty minutes, you risk feeling lethargic afterward or, even worse, oversleeping and missing a class. If you attend a large college or university, be sure to allow adequate time to get from one class to another.

✧ **Try to alternate classes with free periods.** Also, seek out instructors who'll let you attend lectures at alternative times if you're absent. If they offer flexibility in due dates for assignments, all the better.

✧ If you're a commuter student, you might be tempted to schedule your classes in blocks without breaks. But before you do this, consider the following:

- The fatigue factor
- No last-minute study periods before tests
- The possibility of having several exams on the same day
- In case of illness, falling behind in all classes

With your own **biorhythms and preferences** in mind, fill out the following table. Use check marks to match up typical activities with *your* best time of day to do these activities.

	Early morning 3–8 a.m.	Morning 8 a.m.–12 p.m.	Mid-day 12–5 p.m.	Evening 5–11 p.m.	Late night 11 p.m.–3 a.m.
Exercise					
Classes					
Homework					
Appointments					
Errands					
Job					
Socializing					
Laundry, paying bills, etc.					
Sleep					

Control factor: Know what you **can** and **can't** control

When it comes to planning your time, it helps to know the difference between what you can control and what you can't control.

What you can control

♦ **Making good choices.** How often do you say, "I don't have time"? Probably a lot. But truth be told, you have a choice when it comes to most of the major commitments in your life. You also control many of the small decisions that keep you focused on your goals: when you wake up, how much sleep you get, what you eat, how much time you spend studying, and whether you get exercise. So be a woman or man with a plan. If you want something, you'll make time for it.

♦ **Doing your part to succeed.** Go to all your classes; arrive on time; buy all the required textbooks; keep track of your activities; complete every reading and writing assignment on time; take notes in class; and, whenever possible, participate and ask questions.

♦ **Managing your stress levels.** Organization is the key to tranquility and positive thinking. Manage your time well, and you won't be tormented with thoughts of all the things that need doing. Want to avoid unnecessary stress? Plan ahead.

What you can't control

♦ **Knowing how much you'll need to study right off the bat.** Depending on the kind of high school you went to (and the types of courses you took there) and how long it has been since you've had to study, you might be more or less prepared than your college classmates. If your studying or writing skills lag behind, expect to put in a little extra time until you're up to speed.

♦ **Running into scheduling conflicts.** If you find it hard to get the classes you need, you can seek help from a dean, an academic adviser, or someone in the college counseling center.

♦ **Needing a job to help pay your way.** Just follow the experts' rule of thumb: If you're taking a full course-load, do your best to avoid working more than fifteen hours a week. Any more than that and your academic work could suffer.

✦ 2c Four time-wasting habits to avoid

1. Procrastinating   Maybe you're a perfectionist—in which case, avoiding a task might be easier than having to live up to your own very high expectations (or those of your parents or instructors). Maybe you object to the sheer dullness of an assignment, or you think you can learn the material just as well without doing the work. Maybe you even fear success and know just how to subvert it.

None of these qualifies as a valid reason to put off your work. They're just excuses that will get you in trouble. Fortunately, doing tasks you don't like is excellent practice for real life.

Alert: Procrastination is a slippery slope. Research shows that procrastinators are more likely than other people to develop unhealthy habits like excessive alcohol consumption, smoking, insomnia, poor diet, and lack of exercise. Make sure you get these tendencies under control early. Otherwise, you could feel overwhelmed in other aspects of your life, too.

Tricks to Stop Procrastination:

1. **Break big jobs down into smaller chunks.** Spend only a few minutes planning your strategy and then act on it.

2. **Reward yourself** for finishing a task. For example, you might watch your favorite TV show or play a game with your kids or friends.

3. **Find a quiet, comfortable place to work** that doesn't allow for distractions and interruptions. Don't listen to music or keep the TV on. If you study in your room, shut the door.

4. **Treat your study time as a serious commitment.** That means no phone calls, email, text messages, or social media updates. You can rejoin society later.

5. **Consider the consequences if you don't get down to work.** You don't want to let bad habits hamper your ability to achieve good results *and* have a life.

2. Overextending yourself   Although what constitutes a realistic workload varies significantly from one person to another, feeling overextended is a huge source of stress for college students. Being involved in campus life is fun and important, but it's crucial not to let your academic work take a backseat.

- ✦ **Learn to say no—even if it means letting other people down.** Don't be tempted to compromise your priorities.

- ✦ **But don't give up all nonacademic pursuits.** Students who work or participate in extracurricular activities often achieve higher grades than their less active counterparts partly because of the important role that time management plays in their lives.

- ✦ **If you're truly overloaded with commitments and can't see a way out**, you may need to drop a course before the drop deadline. It may seem drastic, but a low grade on your permanent record is even worse. Become familiar with your school's add/drop policy to avoid penalties. If you receive financial aid, keep in mind that in most cases you must be registered for a minimum number of credit hours to be considered a full-time student and maintain your current level of aid.

3. Losing your focus   Some first-year college students lose sight of their goals. They spend their first term blowing off classes and assignments, then either get placed on probation or have to spend years clawing their way back to a decent GPA. So plan your strategy and keep yourself focused and motivated for the long haul.

4. Running late

Punctuality is a virtue. Rolling in late to class or review sessions shows a lack of respect for both your instructors and your classmates.

Arrive early to class and avoid using your phone, texting, doing homework for another class, falling asleep, talking, whispering, or running out to feed a parking meter. Part of managing your time is freeing yourself to focus on the present and on other people who inhabit the present with you. Note: Respecting others is a habit that can work wonders in your career and personal life.

✦ **2d** Two tools to keep you on track

Once you enter college or the working world, you must immediately do the following: Write down everything you need to do; prioritize your tasks; and leave yourself frequent reminders. The good news is that a little up-front planning will make your life infinitely easier and more relaxing. For one thing, you'll be less likely to make mistakes. On top of that, you'll free your brain from having to remember all the things you need to get done so that you can focus on actually doing the work. Two key items will help you plan to succeed.

A planner or calendar   Find out if your campus bookstore sells a planner with important school-specific dates and deadlines already marked. Or, if you prefer to use an online calendar or the one that comes on your smartphone, that's fine too. As you schedule your time, follow a few basic guidelines:

Pick the timeframe that works best for you. If you want a "big picture" sense of how your schedule plays out, try setting up a calendar for the whole term or for the month. For a more detailed breakdown of what you need to accomplish in the near future, a calendar for the week or even the day may be a better fit. If you're keeping your calendar on a smartphone, you can toggle among different views—day, week, and month.

Enter all of your commitments. Once you've selected your preferred timeframe, record your commitments and other important deadlines. These might include your classes, assignment due dates, work hours, family commitments, and so on. Be specific. For instance, "Read Chapter 8 in history" is preferable to "Study history," which is better than simply "Study." Include meeting times and locations, social events, and study time for each class. Take advantage of your smartphone by setting reminders and alerts to keep you on top of all your activities and obligations.

Break large assignments like research projects into smaller bits, such as choosing a topic, doing research, creating an outline, learning necessary computer skills, writing a first draft, and so on. And give yourself deadlines. Estimate how much time each assignment will take you. Then get a jump on it. A good time manager often finishes projects before the actual due dates to allow for emergencies.

Watch out for your toughest weeks during the term. If you find that paper deadlines and test dates fall during the same week or even the same day, you can minimize some of the stress by finding time to finish other assignments early to free up time for study and writing. If there's a major conflict, talk it over with your professor. Professors will be more likely to help you if you talk with them early instead of at the last minute.

Update your planner/calendar frequently. Enter all due dates as soon as you know them. Be obsessive about this.

Check your planner/calendar every day (at the same time of day if that helps you remember). You'll want to review the current week and the next week, too.

When in doubt, turn to a type-A classmate for advice. A hyperorganized friend can be your biggest ally when it comes to making a game plan.

A to-do list The easiest way to remember all the things you need to do is to jot them down on a running to-do list—updating as needed. You can do this on paper or use an online calendar or smartphone to record the day's obligations.

1. **Prioritize.** Rank items on your list in order of importance. Alternatively, circle or highlight urgent tasks.

2. **Every time you complete a task, cross it off the list.**

3. **Move undone items to the top of your next list.**

4. **Start a new to-do list every day or once a week.** It shouldn't be just about academics. Slot in errands you need to run, appointments, emails you need to send, and anything else you need to do that day or week.

Resources

Control of the Study Environment	**www.ucc.vt.edu/stdysk/control.html**
Mind Tools for Getting the Most Out of Your Time	**www.mindtools.com/page5.html**
Mobile Student Planner	**www.istudentpro.com**
Printable Checklists	**www.allfreeprintables.com/checklists/ to-do-lists.shtml**
Student Organizer	**www.primasoft.com/so.htm**

Bibliography

Chandler Project. 11 Aug. 2008, Chandlerproject.org.

Edberg, Henrik. "Why You Should Write Things Down." *The Positivity Blog*, 12 Sept. 2007, www.positivityblog.com/index.php/2007/09/12/why-you-should-write -things-down/.

Gardner, John N., and Betsy O. Barefoot. "Managing Your Time." *Your College Experience: Strategies for Success*, 10th ed., Bedford/St. Martin's, 2012.

CHAPTER 3

College ethics and personal responsibility

As a college student, it's important for you to understand what kinds of behaviors are considered "academic dishonesty" or, more to the point, cheating. Unfortunately, thanks to technology, it's easier than ever for students to cheat. However, it's also much easier for colleges to catch students who cheat. And administrators are cracking down on cheating by making the penalties increasingly harsh.

To complicate matters, there are plenty of students who cheat *without even knowing that they're cheating*. In the past, you may have been one of these students—perhaps because you didn't know or understand the rules about using other people's work. At some schools, teachers and administrators are more lenient with these students, but it's better not to count on that leniency. It's better to know the rules, the consequences, and some strategies for avoiding cheating.

✦ **3a** What is cheating?

Cheating comes in two forms: faking your own work and helping other students fake theirs.

Some of the most obvious forms of cheating

- ✦ Buying an essay from someone else

- ✦ Texting answers during an exam

- ✦ Sharing the details of a test with students who haven't taken it yet

- ✦ Copying someone else's homework

- Peeking at someone else's test paper

- Letting other people cheat from your work

- Stealing a test

- Writing answers to the test in tiny letters on your gum wrappers or on the inside of your bottled water label. (Note: Professors know these tricks.)

Plagiarism: The most common form of cheating

The trouble with plagiarism is that a lot of students don't completely understand what it is. Plagiarism, according to the *Oxford English Dictionary*, is "taking someone else's work or ideas and passing them off as your own."

Does anyone *really* think it's OK to copy whole sentences from the Internet and paste them into their essays? Some people don't think twice about downloading copyrighted music, so it could be that the concepts of *ownership* and *borrowing* aren't as clear as they used to be. Perhaps personal responsibility is muddy when it comes to intellectual property. What's your stance? Have you ever lifted a passage from a website, maybe even changing words to make it sound more like you? Do you believe that once something is on the web, it's in the public domain? Copying or paraphrasing anything from the Internet, or from any another source, and using it without citing the source is cheating.

Beware: Plagiarizing with intent is one thing. Many college students are accused of plagiarism simply because they are being irresponsible and forget to define which parts of an essay are their own and which parts belong to another author. It's in your best interest to seek out your school's plagiarism policy and definitions.

I have viewed and understand my school's plagiarism policy and the consequences of submitting plagiarized work as my own.

Signed: _____ Date: _____

✦ 3b The case for integrity

Cheating is wrong, and it doesn't represent the hard work needed for success in school and beyond. Getting caught could set off a firestorm and seriously affect your future. What's worse, cheating is bad for your self-image and can trigger both guilt and anxiety.

Because attending college is ultimately about learning new things, challenging yourself, and building your integrity, you defeat the whole point if you try to get through dishonestly.

And here's the sobering reality: Cheating has a nasty way of seeping into other parts of your life, like your career, your finances, and your personal relationships, where it can cause long-term damage. But integrity can seep as well. If you conduct your academic life with honesty and integrity and live as a college student with principles, chances are you'll live your life as a person who's seen as honest and principled in your personal and professional environments as well.

✦ 3c Tools teachers use when they suspect cheating

College professors can easily investigate their suspicions, and nowadays they have better resources to back them up. Programs like Turnitin.com let instructors scan essays and crosscheck them against books, newspapers, journals, and student papers, as well as against material that's publicly accessible on the web. Even without such a program, a teacher can put a suspicious passage into a Google search and turn up possible plagiarism. Just a brief, single-sentence snippet could give you away. In short, don't risk getting caught. If you're overwhelmed, meet with your teacher and tell him or her that you're overwhelmed. Or take a trip to the writing center and work through citing sources with one of the tutors. Know some alternatives so that the possibility of getting caught isn't causing you anxiety.

✦ 3d How to be a responsible student: Ten tips

1. **Avoid friends who pressure you to bend the rules.** Writing a paper is really hard. Doing advanced math and science homework is really hard. Studying for exams is lonely, boring, and *really* hard. But trying to beat the system doesn't pay. Remind yourself of the consequences of cheating. Explain to your friends that you are on a valiant quest for honest effort.

2. **Join a study group.** If you're struggling to get through a course, get together with other students to compare notes and help each other grasp tricky concepts. A study group gives you a support system and a more positive belief in yourself. It teaches you persistence and discipline because the group structure involves

meeting promptly at set times for reviews. A study group can also make learning easier and more fun.

3. **Don't procrastinate.** Here's the deal: If you want to write a thorough and honest essay, you need to start early. College papers aren't like movie reviews. You're often required to do lots of outside research. Then you have to read through it all to figure out what's valuable. Next, you have to incorporate the highlights into an outline, a first draft, and ultimately an original work that's all your own. All of that takes time. If you leave things too late, you'll be more tempted to cheat.

4. **Don't muddle your notes.** It's vital that you keep your own writing separate from the material you've gathered from other sources. Why? Because it's surprisingly easy to mistake someone else's words for your own, especially after you get two hours into writing and your brain turns numb. So document everything.

5. **Be a stickler about internal citation.** It happens all the time. At the end of an essay, a student provides a full works cited list, including all the works he or she has quoted, summarized, or paraphrased. But in the paper itself, there are no citations to be found. Using phrases that signal the switch from your idea to a source's idea—along with the page number of the source (if one is available)—can make a big difference. In this example from the body of a student paper, the writer uses internal citation along with a signal phrase.

> Surprisingly, students in reduced meal programs don't always participate. According to a recent report from the Food Research and Action Center, "stigma and the allure of competitive foods" decrease student participation in the program (10).

6. **Familiarize yourself with the proper formatting for a research paper.** The MLA style is widely used in classes such as English and composition; if your instructors require a different style, they will let you know. For learning the basic guidelines and rules for citations, your handbook is an excellent tool. You might also want to speak to a reference librarian, an expert in gathering research and someone who can be one of your biggest allies in college. Alternatively, pay a visit to the writing center on campus or talk to your instructor for advice.

7. **Be sure to list all of the sources you quoted, summarized, or paraphrased in your works cited list.** Sources should be listed alphabetically in proper MLA format. We repeat—if you're not sure how to list a citation or if you're not sure that your source information is valid, don't just put it down and keep your fingers crossed.

8. **Master the art of paraphrasing.** Paraphrasing is restating someone else's ideas or observations in your own words. Paraphrasing involves understanding the original passage and presenting it in your own way. You don't have to put the text in quotation marks, but a citation acknowledging the original source is still required.

9. **If you need help, seek it early.** This sounds obvious, but it's important to go to the writing center or the librarian *well before your paper is actually due.* Proofreading takes time—and chances are, your paper will need a few tweaks.

10. **If you hand something in and then realize that you used material without giving credit to the source, alert your instructor immediately.** Don't just hope it will slip through. Better to risk half a grade point on one essay than your whole college career, right?

✦ 3e How to paraphrase (to avoid plagiarism)

Paraphrasing doesn't mean copying a quotation and switching the words around. It doesn't mean changing two or three words in a sequence, either. It means rephrasing and restructuring someone else's idea altogether while retaining its meaning. Paraphrasing requires you, as a writer, to *understand the author's meaning* and then present it in your own way and in your own sentence structure. Consider these examples:

QUOTATION	"The jobs growth forecast for the auto industry appears dim."
PARAPHRASE	We will see a decrease in the number of available jobs at the biggest carmakers.

QUOTATION	"Google has been working to build cars that drive themselves."
PARAPHRASE	One of Google's latest projects is a robotic car that takes humans out of the driver's seat.

If you're having trouble paraphrasing something, try this strategy: Put away your source material, call up a friend or your mom, and explain the point you're trying to summarize. Chances are you'll come away with something that's clear and concise, that's in your own words, and that reflects your own presentation of the ideas.

When you paraphrase someone else's words, you still have to cite the source.

> TIP
>
> **When copying research material into your notes, write the name of the source and the page number directly after it.** *Likewise, when you copy something from the Internet, add a URL. Use quotation marks around all cited material. Also try highlighting your research in a bright color to set it apart from your notes. All of this will make writing your draft easier.*

PRACTICE ✦ Paraphrase this passage from earlier in this chapter.

> If you're struggling to get through a daunting course, get together with other students to compare notes and help each other grasp tricky concepts. A study group gives you a support system and a more positive belief in yourself. It teaches you persistence and discipline because the group structure involves meeting promptly at set times for reviews. A study group can also make learning easier and more fun.

According to advice by Bedford/St. Martin's, _____

_____

_____

_____

_____

_____

_____ (19).

Bibliography

Feldman, Robert. *The Liar in Your Life: The Way to Truthful Relationships.* Hachette Book Group, 2009, pp. 59–60.

Fishman, Rob. "Beating Cheating." *The Cornell Daily*, 8 Nov. 2006, cornellsun.com/node/19684.

Fleming, Grace. "Cheating: Why It's Different in College." *About.com: Homework/Study Tips*, homeworktips.about.com/od/homeworkhelp/a/collegecheating.htm.

Gabriel, Trip. "Plagiarism Lines Blur for Students in Digital Age." *The New York Times*, 1 Aug. 2010, www.nytimes.com/2010/08/02/education/02cheat.html.

CHAPTER 4

College etiquette

No sensible person wants to go off to college and make a bad impression. Succeeding in college requires having an understanding of college etiquette, the basic rules for behaving and communicating in an academic environment. Your success will rest on your learning to be professional and courteous to teachers, school staff, and peers.

✦ **4a** Four truths

1. **Certain things are expected of you in college.** All institutions of higher education operate under a simple code that requires you to treat your instructors and fellow students as valued contributors to a worthwhile endeavor: namely, your education. It pays to cultivate an interest in them and be polite.

2. **Instructors judge you by your manners.** Your social skills (or lack thereof) get reflected in your grades, in the references professors write on your behalf, and even in the opportunities you're given in college and beyond. Good manners give you an edge by making you seem even more likeable and impressive than you already are.

3. **Knowing exactly what behavior is expected of you will make you a more confident student.** You may have grown up with casual standards at home or in high school, and that can put you at a big disadvantage in college. You don't want to worry about being so inexperienced that you accidentally offend your favorite professor, do you?

4. **Having the right attitude, or mental approach to life, is important.** Happy people tend to be more productive, considerate, and successful than unhappy people. So even if you're taking a required class that seems boring and useless, try to remember why you're in college in the first place. It helps to think in terms of your goals.

✦ **4b** Starting out

Since you never have a second chance to make a first impression, think through how you'll interact with people in your new academic environment.

Err on the side of being too formal.   Being too formal in new college relationships is better than being too casual, which could come off as rude. Listen attentively. Raise your hand before speaking. Say thank you. Reply pleasantly and thoughtfully to questions.

Learn your instructors' names.   The most basic way to charm your teachers and express interest in their courses is to address them properly. Never call your instructors by their first names or nicknames unless they specifically ask you to. It's best to use *Professor* _____, *Dr.* _____, or—if your instructor doesn't have a tenured position—*Mr.* or *Ms.* _____.

TIP | **The Hidden Costs of Texting:** *What's wrong with checking your texts and emails during class once in a while? Good question, and here's the answer: It can actually count against your grade. Some college professors deduct points from a student's overall class participation grade if the student seems more engaged with a phone or other device than with what's going on in class.*

Abandon your phone at the classroom door.   Unless your teacher regularly asks you to use personal phones as response devices during class, make a habit of turning your phone off. And don't just turn the ringer down. *Turn off the phone completely.* You should not check texts during class. You should not play games or use apps on your phone while your instructor is teaching. Cell phone use is the number one etiquette problem in college classes right now.

✦ 4c Classroom rules

Your instructors care about your future and will be willing to meet with you before or after class. However, they aren't accountable for your success or failure. Following a few rules will show that you are prepared to command your own success.

1. **Show up.** Attendance is important. Missing one day in college is like missing a week of high school, because everything is so much more concentrated.

2. **Show up on time.** Plan your commute and arrange your courses so that you can get to class right on schedule. Ideally, you want to arrive a few minutes early, so that you can calmly find a seat and take out your book, laptop, and other supplies.

3. **Come prepared.** If you've been assigned reading or homework, no matter how grueling, have it done in advance.

4. **Pay close attention to the syllabus.** The syllabus spells out exactly what's required of you if you're going to succeed in the class. The syllabus often lists readings, assignments, policies, and the instructor's contact information.

5. **Expect to work.** You're not entitled to a passing grade merely because you show up to class or because you've paid for the credits. To succeed, you need to participate in discussions, take notes, study, do well on tests, and complete all of your assignments. If you're sinking, talk to your professor during office hours. There's an incredible amount of help on college campuses: writing centers, math tutors, language labs for nonnative English speakers, and academic advisers.

6. **Don't surf the web.** Taking notes on your laptop is fine. Checking your email or posting on Twitter is not. These activities distract other students, and professors view such activity as rude.

7. **Don't try to monopolize the conversation.** You're in class to learn something, right? So find a balance between participation in the discussion and active listening. While you're at it, be a great listener in study groups, too.

✦ 4d Collaborating with others: The group project

Today, most college classes involve doing hands-on projects in small groups. The shift to a more learner-centered classroom environment is a response to the idea that classroom demands should, in part, prepare you for workplace demands. Team settings, common in the workplace, involve a new kind of etiquette.

◇ **Treat the students in your group as teammates.** It's vital that you pull your weight, come to meetings on time, listen to what others have to say, and plan together. A group project shouldn't be competitive. You're all pulling toward the same goal, and part of your grade may be based on your teamwork skills.

◇ **Give constructive criticism.** If you're required to offer a peer review of an essay, stay neutral and focused, and don't get personal. It's helpful to use "I"-statements. For example, "I'm confused" is better than "This paper is confusing." Also, it helps to keep to specifics: What did you like best about the essay and why? Where would you like to know more information?

◇ **Prepare to learn from each other.** The fact that the people in your group have different backgrounds and talents—but are interested in the same subject—already makes for a creative group dynamic. Chances are, bouncing ideas off your classmates will make you smarter and broaden your world view.

✦ 4e Communicating with your professor

Most instructors are passionate about their subject matter and really appreciate students. Make a habit of talking with them occasionally outside of class.

1. **Discover office hours.** Almost all instructors post days and times when they're available to students—and if those hours don't work for you, you can always ask to schedule an appointment. Attending office hours is one of the best learning tools you have in college. Visit early in the semester for quick check-ins—don't wait until just before an exam or the due date for an essay.

2. **Embrace your college email account.** Check your college email account often for updates, even if you do not use it regularly in your life outside of school. Your instructors may use the tool to send information about assignments, activities, and canceled classes. Used properly, it can be a great way to communicate with your professor, too.

3. **Don't expect your instructor to call you back after work.** Many college faculty members are careful not to call students back from home because they don't want their private numbers made public and because they don't want to seem unprofessional. If you leave a message for your professor, either by phone or email, it could be a full twenty-four hours before he or she contacts you.

4. **If you have a personal crisis, head to the office for a face-to-face meeting.** If you find yourself in an exceptional situation that is affecting your class work, talk to your instructor in private, not in the classroom with nineteen other people listening. Most teachers will work with you.

Serious mistakes

1. **Disappearing.** It happens more often than you'd think: Students attend class for a couple of weeks and then vanish into thin air. Keep in mind that the college disappearing act can affect your financial aid.

2. **Not staying in touch with your professors.** If you must be away or you have a conflict with an exam, make arrangements with your instructor ahead of time. It's important to do this well in advance.

3. **Blatant rudeness.** Some behavior—chronic lateness, obvious texting, being abusive to other students in a debate—is virtually apology-resistant.

The right way to ask for a reference

✧ **Give your professor two to four weeks' lead-time.** It takes thought and research to write a good reference, and your instructor might have to unearth your file from a few semesters back. Keep in mind that college faculty members are busy people.

✧ **Provide a stamped envelope** (and make sure to use the correct postage). Or if the reference is to be submitted online, be sure to give your professor thorough instructions on how to reach the correct site.

✧ **Be thorough about what the application is for**, what the organization wants to know about you, and where the reference needs to be sent.

Have a complaint?

✧ **Talk to your instructor privately**, during office hours.

✧ **Speak in "I"-messages, not "you"-messages.** "You"-messages ("You never explained this stuff") sound inherently hostile and tend to put people on the offensive. "I"-messages, on the other hand, simply state a problem ("I feel frustrated because we never touched on logical fallacies in class, yet there was a question about it on the test").

✧ **Resist the urge to vent about your professor on the Internet.** Online discussion groups and social websites are not the place to whine about your school, your instructor, or your fellow students. That's what calling home is for. Everything posted to the web is public.

How to write to your professor

These three words can be a simple guideline: Use formal English. Using shorthand or text slang can affect your professor's attitude toward you—and not in a good way. Consider a few examples of actual student emails:

Acceptable:

Dear Professor Fuller,

This is David K. I am in your TR 11:30-12:45 Eng-091 Class. I was unable to attend class this morning due to a bad reaction I had to some food I ate last night. I was in the ER this morning. I was wondering if it is at all possible to know what the lesson was on today and I will work on it during the weekend. I know I will not get credit for it but I would like to work on it anyway.

Thank you,

David

Unacceptable:

hi is april are u gonna send us the homework so i can print it out and show u it

Unacceptable:

Hello Fuller,

I'm sorry to not come today I was just wondering if I can take the gammar test tomorrow in your moring class please. My mom Got Rush to the hospital. I promise I will not miss no more classes. I know this is my third time but im trying to do good. So please can you get back to me asap. Nicki

Being gracious to your academic adviser: A how-to When you visit your academic adviser, you can't present yourself like a blank slate and expect your adviser to sketch out your future. The smart, polite thing to do is to do your homework *before* the meeting. Tell your adviser what classes you're interested in and which majors you're considering. Know your work schedule so that you can pick classes that don't conflict with your job. If you're saying to yourself, "I have no idea which direction to go," spend some time in the career center. Then meet with your academic adviser, ask thoughtful questions, and listen up.

PRACTICE ✦ Rewrite the following email to a professor, using a professional tone, proper formatting, and Standard English. Feel free to invent a name for the professor and any other details you think the message may need.

> Hey i am applying for the dean's team so I can b a mentor for incoming students in the Bus. School. i need a recomendtion from a teacher and you now me well i have a good grade in yr class would you write it thanks! Roberto

_____

_____

_____

_____

_____

_____

_____

_____

_____

_____

Bibliography

Burgess, Heidi. "I-Messages and You-Messages." *Beyondintractability.org*, Oct. 2003, www.beyondintractability.org/essay/I-messages/.

Martin, Judith. *Miss Manners' Guide to Rearing Perfect Children.* Penguin Books, 1985.

Schiller, Emily. "Taking Advantage of Office Hours." *Backtocollege.com*, www.back2college.com/office-hours.htm.

Stafford, Diane. "Study Finds That Happy Workers Are More Productive Workers." *TampaBay.com*, 10 April 2009, www.tampabay.com/news/business/workinglife/article990727.ece.

CHAPTER 5

Developing active reading strategies

Reading in college requires you to read deeply, analyzing what you read for various purposes. Your composition instructor may ask you to analyze a writer's claims and support for an argument, evaluating its effectiveness in convincing readers. A history instructor may assign a research topic, asking you to analyze the major causes of the Civil War and its effects on society today. In your economics class, you may be asked to write a paper in which you compare the theories of two prominent economists.

✦ 5a On-ramps for reading assignments

The better you understand a reading, the better prepared you will be to handle academic reading and writing assignments. It may be tempting to skip the reading and go straight to writing or to read just the first page or two of an article, but without a clear understanding of the assigned reading or the sources you gather at the library, you will have difficulty completing your academic assignments successfully.

The following strategies will help you dig in to what you read. The particular strategy steps you use will depend on your reading task. With practice, you will gain confidence and efficiency in choosing and using effective, active reading strategies. Think of deep strategic reading as looking for on-ramps to a reading that will help you understand it. Not all readings will require the same on-ramps, so you will have to be flexible. You may need to approach one reading differently than you approach another. Your goal, of course, is to understand a reading from start to finish.

This chapter covers five on-ramps for active, strategic reading:

✦   Pay attention to titles.

✦   Read for patterns.

- ✧   Understand vocabulary.

- ✧   Identify main ideas.

- ✧   Outline what you read.

✦ **5b** Pay attention to titles

Titles give readers their first clues to the writer's purpose, audience, and thesis. Consider the following titles carefully. With a partner, describe what you expect to read about. (See additional activities on page 123.)

a.   "Growing Global Water Scarcity Creates a New Breed of Criminal: Will You Become One?"

_____

_____

b.   "Parenting Styles Linked to Teen Distracted Driving"

_____

_____

c.   "How Suburban Landscaping Is Increasing Disease-Carrying Populations of Mosquitoes and Why Solutions Are Costly to Pursue"

_____

_____

Note: You should also learn as much as you can about the publication in which a reading appears, the publication date, and the author. Information about the publication and the author provides added clues to the writer's purpose and intended audience. You should reflect on the publication date, considering how the issue may have changed since the piece was written.

ACTIVITY ✦ Using a title as an on-ramp

Find an article on a local or national news website (NPR, CNN, _The Washington Post_). Copy the name of the article here, but don't read the article.

_____

With just the title and the publication in mind, describe what you expect to read about.

_____

_____

✦ 5c Read for patterns

Writers organize their ideas into logical patterns to communicate the ideas clearly to readers. Narration is one logical pattern. A narrative is often organized chronologically (that is, in order by time): beginning, middle, and end. Reading for patterns will help you follow the logic of what you read.

Consider the following patterns and transition words/phrases that writers, you included, rely on to organize ideas. Think of finding patterns in a writer's work as reverse analysis. Everything you read was written by someone who had to decide how to organize ideas in a way that readers would understand.

Pattern	How the pattern unlocks the writer's purpose	Key questions to consider when reading a work with this pattern	Typical transition words
Narration	Lets a writer tell a story or show how events unfold in time order	What are the events of the story? Why is this story being told?	first, second, as, during, after, next, meanwhile, finally, when, while
Description	Provides details that bring a person, place, or thing to life	What details and language are being used and why? What is the emotional or sensory impact of this description?	above, below, beyond, near, nearby, in, inside, similarly, likewise
Illustration	Supports an idea, argument, or proposal with examples	How does this illustration make things clear to me?	for example, for instance, in particular, to illustrate, in other words, in fact, specifically
Classification	Sorts people, things, or ideas into categories	What are the categories? Is this the way I would group these subjects?	first, second, finally, similarly, likewise, however, on one hand, on the other hand, but, although

Pattern	How the pattern unlocks the writer's purpose	Key questions to consider when reading a work with this pattern	Typical transition words
Definition	Puts a thing or idea in a general class and adds details to distinguish it from others in its class	What is the general class? Do the details give me a better sense of what this thing or idea is?	for example, and, but, however
Process	Describes a process or shows readers, step by step, how to do something	What are the steps? Are the steps clear and logical?	first, next, then, after, as, while, when, meanwhile, finally
Compare/ Contrast	Lets a writer show how two people, places, things, or ideas are similar to and/or different from each other	What similarities/ differences are being listed? What seems important about these similarities/ differences?	also, and, similarly, likewise, but, yet, however, on the other hand, in contrast, even though
Cause/Effect	Shows the factors that led to or might lead to an outcome or shows the possible results of a certain cause	What reasons or factors are given? What positive or negative outcomes are listed?	therefore, if, so, for, thus, because, since

Note: Writers seldom use only one pattern to organize their ideas for readers. (Anticipate that more than one pattern is being employed. And when you are writing, challenge yourself to use more than one pattern in brainstorming and organizing your ideas as well.)

ACTIVITY ✦ Using patterns as an on-ramp

Label patterns in the margin of your reading and use them to explain the writer's point. See page 124 for readings you can practice with.

✦ 5d Understand vocabulary

Throughout your reading process, make the time to look up words you don't know. To save time and effort, have dictionary.com open when you read so that you can look up words quickly. If more than one definition is offered, consider which definition best fits the sentence. Write that definition in the margin or in the space above the word. Strong readers generally take the time to look up words they do not know, and over time they increase their vocabulary.

A popular timesaver is to search for context clues—clues to a word's definition, found in the sentence where the word occurs or the sentences around it. Use context clues to determine the definition of the word *reminisce* in this passage from "My Pilgrimage" by student Jasen Berverly.

> Upon reaching Downtown Crossing at 7:45, I exit the train and begin to watch as people dart down the long corridor in hopes of catching the train. This becomes the highlight of the morning as I watch the doors slam in people's faces. There's no explaining the humor of watching people who have tried so hard, panting angrily as the train leaves without them.
>
> Standing on the platform, I recognize a few familiar faces. They belong to students of Charlestown High School. I laugh, knowing that school for them began at 7:20. Then I begin to reminisce about my own CHS experiences. I think about all my suspension hearings, the work I refused to do, and how easy it was to get by doing the bare minimum. Only the cold draft of the approaching train brings me back to reality.

The following sentence provides the clue that *to reminisce* means to think about one's past: "I think about all my suspension hearings, the work I refused to do, and how easy it was to get by doing the bare minimum."

ACTIVITY ✦ Using vocabulary as an on-ramp

Fill the spaces between lines of text with definitions of words you don't know. Underline or circle clues to difficult or technical terms. See page 126 for readings you can practice with.

✦ **5e** Identify main ideas

Consider how paragraphs begin and end. Note that the first or last sentence in a paragraph often presents the overall idea of the paragraph. Understanding the main idea in each paragraph will give you clues about the major idea or ideas in a complete reading. Consider this paragraph from a chapter on post–Revolutionary War America in a history textbook.

> **While women's influence was praised in the post–Revolutionary era, state laws rarely expanded women's rights. All states limited women's economic autonomy, although a few allowed married women to enter into business. Divorce was also legalized in many states but was still available only to the wealthy and well connected. Meanwhile women were excluded from juries, legal training, and, with rare exceptions, voting rights.**
>
> Source: Hewitt, Nancy A., and Steven F. Lawson. *Exploring American Histories*, 2nd ed., Bedford/St. Martin's, p. 160.

This paragraph gives some sense of what women's lives were like in the early days of our nation. You may suspect that the larger reading addresses the growing influence of women in America, even with the limitations mentioned in this paragraph.

ACTIVITY ✦ Using main ideas as an on-ramp

Challenge yourself to mark or write down the main idea of each paragraph. You may decide that two or more paragraphs work as a unit to convey one main point. See chapter 14 for readings you can practice with.

✦ **5f** Outline what you read

Another active reading strategy is to create an outline in the margins that labels the content of the reading from start to finish (main idea, important evidence, "reason #2," or good data point, for example). These notes will be helpful when you prepare for a class discussion of the article, when you look for quotations from the article for an essay you're writing, or when you begin studying for a quiz or exam that includes information from the reading.

ACTIVITY ✦ Using outlining as an on-ramp

Create an outline in the margins of an article you have been assigned to read. See chapter 14 for readings you can practice with.

✦ 5g One additional strategy: Converse with a reading

To converse is to participate in a conversation. When you read actively, you imagine that you are in a conversation with the author. You're not just noting the main ideas, but actually responding to them — sometimes politely and sometimes with strength or passion, depending on how you feel about the topic. Conversing with a text involves asking questions, calling attention to ideas that don't make sense, and beginning to draw conclusions from the author's words and ideas.

A double-entry notebook can help you to have an academic conversation with a text and its author. On one side of the notebook page, you write words, phrases, or sentences from the original text. On the other side of the page, you list your questions about, your conclusions about, and your challenges to what you've read.

The following is a brief excerpt from Barbara Ehrenreich's *Bright-sided*, a book in which the experienced journalist questions the power of positive thinking.

> **Americans are a "positive" people. This is our reputation as well as our self-image. We smile a lot and are often baffled when people from other cultures do not return the favor. In the well-worn stereotype, we are upbeat, cheerful, optimistic, and shallow, while foreigners are likely to be subtle, world-weary, and possibly decadent. American expatriate writers like Henry James and James Baldwin wrestled with and occasionally reinforced this stereotype, which I once encountered in the 1980s in the form of a remark by Soviet émigré poet Joseph Brodsky to the effect that the problem with Americans is that they have "never known suffering." (Apparently he didn't know who had invented the blues.) Whether we Americans see it as an embarrassment or a point of pride, being positive—in affect, in mood, in outlook—seems to be engrained in our national character.**

Source: Ehrenreich, Barbara. Bright-sided: How the Relentless Promotion of Positive Thinking Has Undermined America, Henry Holt, 2009, p. 1.

Here is a sample double-entry notebook page about Ehrenreich's passage.

Ideas from the text	My responses/questions
"Americans are a 'positive' people. . . . In the well-worn stereotype, we are upbeat, cheerful . . ." (1).	Where I come from, the Midwest, we are generally friendly and cheerful and what could be called positive. The author puts quotation marks around "positive" and uses the phrase "well-worn stereotype," which makes me think she actually doesn't think we're all that positive or that, if we are, she doesn't really value it.
"Whether we Americans see it as an embarrassment or a point of pride, being positive . . . seems to be engrained in our national character" (1).	The author seems to be restating the stereotype here but also hinting that there is some debate about it—an interesting idea. Who would see positive thinking as an "embarrassment" or as a negative characteristic? Anyway, it could hint at some disagreement about how we see ourselves or how we want to be seen by others.

ACTIVITY ✦ Using conversing as an on-ramp

For something you have been assigned to read, create three or four notebook entries in which you talk back to the author of the reading. See pages 129–130 for an article you can practice with.

CHAPTER 6

Strengthening peer review and collaboration skills

Writing is often a social process. The people around you can provide ideas and insights that you had not considered on your own. In college and beyond, your writing will benefit if you work with others, either through peer review or by collaborating on a project. With peer review, you share your work with others, gather their feedback, and use it to revise your writing effectively. You also act as a reviewer for your peers, helping them improve their drafts. In a collaborative project, you work with others from the start to complete a piece of writing or other project. Working collaboratively requires a different composing process than writing on your own. This chapter offers tips on how to work with others effectively, either during peer review or while collaborating on a project.

✦ 6a What is peer review?

Since it can be difficult to spot errors, gaps, and weaknesses in your own writing, revising alone is often not enough. Instead, once you finish a draft, you might ask one or more peers—classmates, friends, or writing tutors—to read it and offer feedback. In other words, you might ask them to engage in peer review. They can help you see your paper through your audience's eyes, pinpoint what's working and what isn't, and give you advice on how to improve it. You can do the same for your peers' writing. Your professor may ask you to do peer review in class, or you may seek out reviewers on your own.

REFLECTION ✦ Your experience with peer review

Think of a time when a classmate, a friend, or another reviewer gave feedback on your writing that was particularly helpful. Do you remember the feedback?

Why do you think it was so helpful? How did you change your writing based on that person's comments?

✎

_____

_____

_____

_____

✦ 6b Tips for offering feedback to a peer

The tips below can help you provide useful, constructive feedback when reviewing a peer's writing.

- ✦ **Focus on global issues.** Give feedback tied to the writer's overall goal for the paper, rather than sentence-level issues. Instead of focusing on grammar, word choice, or spelling, think about the "big picture." Is the writer's purpose clear? Does the writer have enough support for the thesis? Do you understand the writer's argument? Is the essay organized logically?

- ✦ **Take notes.** As you read through an essay, make notes to guide your feedback later. Identify the writer's argument and supporting points to make sure you understand them. You may also want to make notes on the paper itself, such as a question mark (?) next to sections that confuse you or a plus sign (+) next to sections where you'd like more detail. Remember, you are not an editor; avoid proofreading the essay or correcting grammar as you read.

- ✦ **Think of yourself as a coach, not a judge.** Think of the peer review session as a dialogue. Ask questions, offer suggestions, and let the writer decide how to use your advice.

  NO   _You should rewrite this paragraph to say _____._

  YES   _Try reorganizing this paragraph to make your point clearer._

- ✦ **Make your comments specific.** Although you are focusing on big-picture issues, your feedback should be clear, specific, and personal. Try using "I"-statements to explain what you think, and follow each statement with your reasoning so that the writer understands why you think that way. Or give a specific suggestion if you have one, coaching the writer and not dictating changes.

  NO   _Your conclusion is confusing._

  YES   _I was confused by your conclusion because _____._

  YES   _Consider rewriting your conclusion so that it connects back to your thesis._

ACTIVITY ✦ Giving peer review comments

Imagine that Alex, the writer of the following rough draft, has come to you for advice about revising his essay. What will you tell him? Write your feedback next to his draft and/or on the lines below. Remember to focus on global issues (argument, organization, appeals), not grammar or punctuation, which Alex plans to correct after making his global revisions.

If you are concerned enough about the earths environment to make six easy steps a part of your regular routine, your individual actions can help save the planet for this generation and the generations to come.

First of all, people who want to help the planet can recycle. Recycling includes more than cans, bottles, and newspapers. Adopt your grandparents' attitude about reusing things. Don't throw out that lamp, but pass it on to someone else. Pass down clothing from one child to the next. A person concerned about the environment looks at everything before he puts it in the trash can, and asks himself, could someone use that item? If the answer is yes, don't throw it away.

Another thing you can do is conserve energy. That doesn't mean loafing in the hammock all day. It means turning off lights and computers and tv's when not using them. It means planning your errands so that you make one trip instead
of three or four. It means biking or taking public transportation instead of driving to class or to your job. Another way to help is to replace as much of the plastic you use as you can. Does your office or church use styrofoam cups for coffee? Paper may cost more, but its easier on the planet. You might even go all the way and use a ceramic cup that you can reuse endlessly. The only chore that would add to your day would be washing a cup. Is the planet worth that much of your time?

Finally, you can replace some of what you've used. Plant a tree. Cultivate a garden. Grind up the leaves in your yard and compost them to replace the soil. If everyone did these few things, life on our planet would be much safer for all.

_____

_____

_____

_____

_____

_____

_____

✦ **6c** Tips for working with feedback from a peer

While feedback from your peers is helpful, you might have trouble incorporating it into your writing. The following tips will help you use peer comments to revise your draft effectively.

✧ **Guide your reviewers.** Before you give your paper to reviewers, explain your intended purpose, your main ideas, and some background on your topic. If you have specific concerns, let your reviewers know what those are. To focus their feedback and let them know where to begin, try starting them off with a few questions you have ("Do I support my thesis well?" "In this paragraph, I want to make the point that _____. Is my point clear?").

✧ **Treat peer review as a dialogue.** Once you have feedback, ask questions about any comments that confuse you. If a reviewer gives feedback that's too general, ask why he or she feels that way or ask the person to point to examples in your paper. You may even want to run changes by your reviewers to see if you've addressed their concerns.

✧ **Keep an open mind.** When someone critiques your writing, it's easy to get defensive. Remember that a reviewer's feedback is meant to help you, not to attack you or your paper. Instead of taking negative feedback personally, consider why readers feel the way they do and what you can change to strengthen the writing. This more positive outlook will help you become a better writer.

✧ **Weigh the feedback.** If you have multiple reviewers, you may be faced with more proposed changes than you can realistically make, or even comments that conflict with each other. As you sort through feedback, keep your essay's purpose in mind. Focus on the comments that will best help you reach your goals for the assignment and that address global issues instead of small ones.

✦ **6d** What is collaboration?

As a college writer, you may collaborate on a project with a partner or group. Instead of writing on your own and then gathering your peers' feedback, you will need to work with peers through every step of the process—brainstorming, researching, drafting, revising, designing, and perhaps even presenting. Collaborative work gives you an opportunity to explore ideas and practices that your peers bring to the project. It's also valuable practice for work you will do outside of school. Many professional projects are done in teams.

REFLECTION ✦ **Your experiences with collaboration**

Think about the last time you completed collaborative work, such as a report, a presentation, or another group project. How was the process different from working on a project on your own? What worked well, and what didn't?

✎ _____

_____

_____

_____

_____

✦ 6e Tips for collaborating effectively

While composing with others can be enriching, doing it effectively takes practice. Below are a few tips for collaborating effectively.

◇ **Do the work together, and learn from each other.** Sometimes students look at collaborative work as just a matter of divvying up tasks (one person does the research, another does the writing, another designs the final document and adds citations). Managing a project this way can result in work that looks like Frankenstein's monster—lots of pieces stitched together into a messy whole. If you work together on every aspect of the project, you will have a stronger, more coherent final product. This approach also will allow you and your team members to learn from one another.

◇ **Organize yourselves, and stay on task.** Functioning well as a group means checking in often and planning together. Here are three ways to keep your group focused and make progress:

1. Set up specific meeting times.

2. Assign someone to take notes when you meet as a group (an ongoing Google doc works well for this).

3. Make sure everyone knows who's doing what for the project.

◇ **Know your own strengths, and be ready to admit your weaknesses.** One way to start, especially if you're working with classmates you don't know well, is to think about how you typically like to work in a team or a group. What are you good at? What do you need to improve? Knowing who is best at what can help you assign roles and divide work effectively.

ACTIVITY ✦ Assess your strengths as a collaborator

Your responses to the questionnaire below can help you and your collaborators get to know one another and start a conversation about how to move forward on your project.

I am good at being a **team organizer**.	yes	no	kind of
I am good at being a **team member**.	yes	no	kind of
I am good at **communication** (asking questions, facilitating discussions, emailing the instructor).	yes	no	kind of
I am good at thinking about the **big picture** (staying focused on the main idea or goal of the project).	yes	no	kind of
I am good at thinking about **small details** (completing individual tasks and keeping track of smaller parts of the project).	yes	no	kind of
I am good at doing **research** (performing web searches, gathering information from library databases, and conducting surveys or interviews with people).	yes	no	kind of
I am good at **design** work (working with or creating images or thinking about layouts and color schemes).	yes	no	kind of
I am good at **writing** (brainstorming, drafting, and editing written materials).	yes	no	kind of
I have good **technology** skills (creating basic web pages, making slide show presentations, and working with video).	yes	no	kind of

CHAPTER 7

Outlining and planning your writing

To help you plan a logical, appealing piece of writing, draft an informal or formal outline near the beginning of your process. Doing so can help you see your organization at a glance—and can even help you spot parts of the essay that might need additional evidence.

✦ 7a Using an informal outline to plan

Informal outlines can take many forms. Perhaps the most common is simply a thesis (or working thesis), followed by a list of major ideas.

SAMPLE INFORMAL OUTLINE

Hawaii is losing its cultural identity.

- **pure-blooded Hawaiians increasingly rare**
- **native language diluted, discouraged**
- **native people forced off ancestral lands**
- **little emphasis on native culture in schools**
- **customs exaggerated and distorted by tourism**

If you begin by jotting down a list of ideas, you can turn the list into a rough outline by crossing out some ideas, adding others, and putting the ideas in a logical order.

ACTIVITY ✦ Now, create your own informal outline for an essay you have been assigned to write.

Working thesis: ✎ _____

_____

- _____

  _____

- _____

  _____

- _____

  _____

- _____

  _____

- _____

  _____

- _____

  _____

Take a moment to review your work and think about how this piece of writing might take shape. Reflect on both your *opportunities* and your *challenges* in developing an essay from this outline. And, of course, start to plan your next steps with your due date in mind.

What are your strongest details, pieces of evidence, or lines of reasoning?

_____

_____

About which part of the outline do you feel most confident?

_____

_____

For what parts will you need to find additional information?

_____

_____

✦ 7b Using a formal outline to plan

Early in the writing process, rough outlines have certain advantages: They can be produced quickly, they are obviously tentative, and they can be revised easily. However, a formal outline may be useful later in the writing process, after you have written a rough draft, especially if your topic is complex. It can help you see whether the parts of your essay work together and whether your essay's structure is logical.

The following formal outline helped its writer improve and clarify the structure of his rough draft. Notice that the student's thesis is an important part of the outline. Everything else in the outline supports it, directly or indirectly. In the following outline, you see two levels of support: major points that directly support the thesis (I, II, III, IV) and minor points that support the major points (A, B, C).

SAMPLE FORMAL OUTLINE

Thesis: Although various methods for disposing of environmental waste have been proposed, each has serious drawbacks.

I. **Antarctic ice sheet disposal is problematic for both scientific and legal reasons.**

    A. **Our understanding of the behavior of ice sheets, especially in an era of climate change, is still too limited.**

    B. **An international treaty prohibits disposal in Antarctica.**

II. **Space disposal is unthinkable.**

    A. **The risk of an accident and worldwide impact is too great, most notably in the case of severely toxic waste.**

    B. **The cost is prohibitive.**

    C. **The method would be unpopular both in the U.S. and abroad.**

III. **Seabed disposal is unwise because we don't know enough about the procedure or its short- and long-term impact.**

    A. **Scientists have not yet solved several technical difficulties.**

    B. **We do not fully understand the impact of such disposal on the ocean's ecology.**

IV. **Deep underground disposal endangers public safety and creates political problems.**

    A. **Geologists disagree about the safest sites, and no sites are completely safe.**

    B. **Political pressure is mounting from citizens who do not want their neighborhoods and states to become toxic dumps.**

    C. **Even with waste that is deemed nontoxic, current plans unfairly target low-income communities.**

How to construct a formal outline   In constructing a formal outline, keep the following guidelines in mind.

1. Put the thesis or working thesis at the top.

2. Make items at the same level of generality as parallel as possible.

3. Use sentences unless phrases are clear.

4. Use the conventional system of numbers and letters for the levels of generality.

> I.
>
>> A.
>>
>> B.
>>
>>> 1.
>>>
>>> 2.
>>>
>>>> a.
>>>>
>>>> b.

5. Always include at least two subdivisions for a category. In other words, before you go to a sublevel, be sure you have at least two subpoints to support the point you are making.

6. Be flexible. Be prepared to revise your outline as your drafts evolve.

Here is an outline template with two levels of support.

Thesis statement: 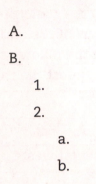 _____

_____

_____

> I.   _____
>
> _____
>
>> A.   _____
>>
>> _____
>>
>> B.   _____
>>
>> _____
>>
>> C.   _____
>>
>> _____

II. _____

_____

A. _____

_____

B. _____

_____

C. _____

_____

III. _____

_____

A. _____

_____

B. _____

_____

C. _____

_____

Here is an outline template with three levels of support.

Thesis statement: _____

_____

_____

I. _____

_____

A. _____

_____

1. _____

_____

2. _____

_____

B. _____

    _____

    1. _____

       _____

    2. _____

       _____

C. _____

    _____

    1. _____

       _____

    2. _____

       _____

II. _____

    _____

A. _____

    _____

    1. _____

       _____

    2. _____

       _____

B. _____

    _____

    1. _____

       _____

    2. _____

       _____

C. _____

    _____

    1. _____

       _____

    2. _____

       _____

III. _____

_____

   A. _____

_____

     1. _____

_____

     2. _____

_____

   B. _____

_____

     1. _____

_____

     2. _____

_____

   C. _____

_____

     1. _____

_____

     2. _____

_____

✦ 7c Using headings to plan

When drafting a research paper or a business document, consider using headings to guide your planning and to help your readers follow the organization of your final draft. While drafting, you can experiment with possible headings, typing chunks of text beneath each heading. You may need to try grouping your ideas in a few different ways to suit your purpose and audience.

The following is a list of headings one student created in an attempt to bring order to her ideas about opioid use among college students. After doing some initial research, she tried to imagine her final document and the organization that would best help her readers to understand the issue. She then used this plan to help her conduct additional research.

SAMPLE HEADINGS FOR A COLLEGE PAPER

Opioid use on college campuses

Use among college athletes

Use among college non-athletes

Effects on academic performance

Effects on athletic performance

Effects on social life

Treatment options

Prevention programs

Call to action

✦ 7d Using a map to plan

Some people are more visual than others. If you are a visual learner or planner, mapping or clustering may work well for you. Mapping emphasizes both relationships among ideas and the hierarchy, or different levels, of your points and subpoints.

Imagine that each circle in the following diagram contained an idea or a piece of evidence. Then the diagram would show one major point or claim, supporting points or subclaims, and a host of details related to the subclaims.

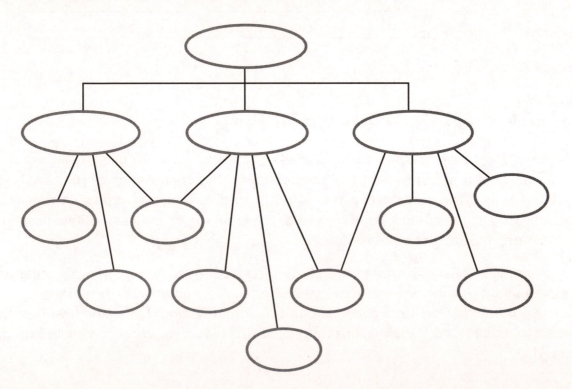

CHAPTER 8

Writing for an audience

When you write academic essays, do you ever consider who your audience is? Of course you are writing for your instructor, right? But it's likely that he or she isn't your only audience.

✦ 8a The link between audience and purpose

All essays need to demonstrate **audience awareness**. At its most basic level, audience awareness means paying attention to the person or group that will read your essay or the person or group to whom you are making an appeal. Audiences have needs and expectations related to your essay, and those needs and expectations may vary from audience to audience. This means that audience and **purpose** (why you are writing to that audience) are closely linked.

Obviously, your teacher will read and ultimately grade your essay. So, what are your teacher's needs and expectations regarding your essay? Regardless of the subject, your essay should show that you are knowledgeable about the subject, can clearly communicate your ideas, and can write in grammatically accurate, error-free sentences. Those are expectations that all teachers will have, in addition to any expectations related to specific requirements or guidelines for the assignment.

If, like many composition courses, your class involves peer review workshops, in which one or more classmates will review your essay and offer feedback, then your teacher is not your only audience. You can consider your peers (classmates) to be part of your audience as well.

✦ 8b Specific and specialized audiences

You may be asked to address a **target audience**, a specific group of readers whose characteristics will affect what you write and how you write it. For example, some professors ask students to write on the same subject to two different audiences to show how audience affects their essay. Imagine writing an essay in which you argue that your state should ban smoking in all public spaces; imagine addressing your argument to a group of *nonsmokers*. Then imagine that your instructor assigned you to argue for the same ban but to address *smokers*. Your purpose or reason for writing would be the same, but your readers would differ. Would you make the same arguments? Would anything change about the way you presented your points? Knowing your audience can help you determine the most successful way to write your essay.

A **specialized audience**, one with a certain technical expertise, may require a different approach than a broader audience. For example, you could aim your appeal for more regular clean-up of local streams and rivers to a general civic audience, to a specific audience of county administrators, or to a specialized audience of environmental scientists.

✦ 8c Thinking about content, tone, vocabulary, and exigence

Effective audience awareness can influence many different elements of your essay, such as content, tone, vocabulary, and exigence.

Content: Some readers will need more detail than others. For example, if you were writing about climate change and addressing your classmates (who cannot be expected to have any in-depth knowledge of your topic), you would need to include background information to help readers understand the subject. You might need to define terms such as *carbon footprint* or describe a process such as the *greenhouse effect*. But a more knowledgeable audience (a group of environmental scientists) would not need such background information. In fact, knowledgeable readers may not want you to include information they consider unnecessary; they may perceive it as wasting their time. Conversely, general readers may not appreciate being confronted with a lot of unfamiliar technical terms and complex concepts that are not explained.

Tone: Tone, the attitude or feeling conveyed by the author, will change depending on the audience. When addressing friends, you may choose to use an informal, conversational tone; however, when addressing other scholars, you may adopt a more formal, academic tone. If, for example, you were writing about a topic such as the death penalty, you would not want to adopt a casual, light-hearted tone because your readers would assume that you were not serious about your subject.

These two sample sentences contain the same content but communicate different tones. Can you tell the difference?

> **Some foolish people mistakenly feel that climate change is not an important issue, but they are totally wrong, and scientific evidence proves that those people don't know what they're talking about!**

> **While some people argue that climate change is not an important issue, there is scientific evidence that proves climate change does actively affect the environment.**

While both sentences emphasize the importance of climate change, the first has a disrespectful tone; the writer suggests that anyone who disagrees is idiotic. Such a tone is likely to alienate readers who have a different viewpoint. In addition, the use of contractions ("don't," "they're") creates an informal tone that is not usually appropriate for academic essays. The second sentence makes the same point about the importance of climate change, yet maintains a respectful and academic tone. It acknowledges that people can disagree on a subject without resorting to insults. Which one of the two sentences would prompt you to keep reading?

Vocabulary: Knowledgeable audiences are likely to be comfortable with **jargon** (technical, subject-specific terms) and can handle elevated **diction** (the level of formality of words). General readers prefer a lower level of diction and may need to have technical terms defined. While it is likely that a group of college-level biology students would be familiar with terms like *allele* and *cytoplasm*, you could not expect a general audience to understand such terminology without explanation.

Exigence: Exigence is an urgency or need that must be addressed. Your goal is to get your readers interested in your topic, since interested readers are more likely to pay attention to the points you are trying to make in your essay. To establish exigence in your essay, you must answer a basic question: Why should your readers care about your topic? Your handbook refers to this as the "So what?" test. Why does your topic matter to your readers? Notice that asking this question is different from asking why you yourself care about the topic. You need to be able to explain why your readers need or want to know about your subject. The exigence may vary for different members of your audience. For example, if your topic is state parks, some readers may care about having enough recreational spaces while others may be more concerned about the costs of creating and maintaining park areas. If you can identify what matters to your audience, you can generate interest by addressing those issues.

Once you have pinpointed your target audience, the next step is to develop strategies to identify that audience's key characteristics.

✦ 8d Questions to help identify audience characteristics

While it is difficult to completely identify your audience (there are so many variables, such as culture, age, knowledge level, and beliefs), you can gain a clearer picture by trying to answer some basic questions.

✧ **What do you already know about your readers?** Can you identify their age range, education level, or expectations about the essay?

_____

_____

✧ **What is their level of knowledge?** What do readers already know about your topic? What will they need to know in order to understand your points? Will they be familiar with technical terms/ideas, or will those terms/ideas need to be explained?

_____

_____

✧ **What are your readers' current attitudes toward your topic?** Will readers generally agree with your point of view or be resistant to your ideas?

_____

_____

✧ **If you are taking a position on your topic, what weaknesses will readers find in your argument? Why (and how) might they oppose your viewpoint?** What specific arguments might they disagree with? What counterargument might they be able to make to refute your point?

_____

_____

♢ **What values, beliefs, or assumptions about your topic does your audience hold? Are there common links between you and your readers?** If you can find connections between your own attitudes toward your topic and those of your readers, you can show them how your essay relates to their interests, which can make them much more receptive to what you have to say.

_____

_____

You may not be able to answer all of these questions fully. At best, your goal is to make an informed estimate of your audience's characteristics. But the more aware you are of your target audience, the better you will be able to tailor your essay to fit their needs and expectations.

✦ **8e** Comparing sample paragraphs

To illustrate the value of audience awareness in composition, consider the following two paragraphs, both intended to introduce the subject of climate change. Which one seems more appropriate for an academic essay? Why?

PARAGRAPH 1

Some folks say that we don't hurt the planet with our actions. Others think we do. No doubt there's a ton of crazy weather these days, right? Hurricanes, blizzards, tornadoes, floods, giant ocean waves crashing over the coast, and who knows what else. Nature's playing some nasty tricks on us! So we need to get to the bottom of it all and figure out what's causing all this craziness. Are we responsible for climate change or is it just a natural thing that would happen no matter what? I think we must be a least part of the problem because of all the cars we drive and exhaust from factories.

PARAGRAPH 2

There are conflicting arguments about the cause of climate change in our society. While some people argue that humans are responsible for climate change due to the overuse of resources such as fossil fuels, others argue that any such changes are simply part of the Earth's natural weather cycles. While it is undeniable that extreme weather conditions, such as hurricanes, tornadoes, blizzards, and floods, seem to be more prevalent these days, what is less certain is the cause of these phenomena. While the cause is debatable, there is ample evidence to indicate that humans are at least partly responsible for climate change due to an overreliance on fossil fuels and the resulting carbon emissions.

Both paragraphs discuss similar ideas; they both provide a general introduction to an ongoing debate about climate change and its causes. But does one paragraph seem more appropriate and effective for its target audience? Paragraph 1 creates an informal tone, uses slang and colloquial vocabulary, and seems more suited for a casual conversation with friends. Furthermore, its use of first-person point of view throughout personalizes the argument rather than suggesting objectivity. Paragraph 2 maintains a more formal tone, uses more elevated diction, and more clearly targets an academic audience. The use of third-person point of view helps establish a level of credibility and objectivity appropriate for its subject and audience.

Audience awareness is an essential component of an academic essay. Accurately identifying your target audience allows you to shape your essay to meet your readers' needs and expectations, creating a more effective essay overall. When preparing to write an essay, always take the time to ask yourself, "Who are my readers and why am I writing to them?"

ACTIVITY ✦ Making adjustments for audience

Choose one of the following topics and briefly (2–3 sentences) explain how you would adjust tone, content, vocabulary, and exigence to address each listed audience.

1. Do violent video games cause violence in society?

    a. Attendees at a video game convention

    b. Group of concerned parents

    _____

    _____

    _____

    _____

2. A discussion of the effects of climate change

    a. Elementary school students learning about environmental science for the first time

    b. High school science club

    _____

    _____

    _____

    _____

3. The impact of social media

    a. Teenagers who are active on Instagram

    b. School counselors and psychologists

    _____

    _____

    _____

    _____

ACTIVITY ✦ Crafting an approach to your audience

For each topic listed below, identify a target audience and plan your approach. How would you adjust tone, vocabulary, content, and exigence appropriately? Briefly explain your reasons for your choices.

1. Establishing good study habits in college

    a. Tone: _____

    _____

    b. Vocabulary: _____

    _____

    c. Content: _____

    _____

    d. Exigence: _____

    _____

2. Preparing to get your driver's license

    a. Tone: _____

    _____

    b. Vocabulary: _____

    _____

    c. Content: _____

    _____

    d. Exigence: _____

    _____

3. Conducting a job search after graduation

   a. Tone: _____

   _____

   b. Vocabulary: _____

   _____

   c. Content: _____

   _____

   d. Exigence: _____

   _____

ACTIVITY ✦ Revising for audience awareness

Revise the following paragraphs, adjusting the content, tone, vocabulary, and exigence to make the paragraph more appropriate for the stated target audience.

1. Topic: Writing an essay in an English composition course

   Audience: Incoming first-year writers at the college

   To write an acceptable essay, students will need to exemplify the highest standards of prose. One must exhibit superior grammatical proficiency, superb communicative capability, and a knowledgeable demeanor. In order to produce the most desirable final product, one only need adhere closely to the three most imperative components of the writing process: prewriting (brainstorming), drafting, and revising. One must also be supremely cognizant of the importance of audience awareness. With those facets in mind, students will achieve the maximum anticipated result: a well-crafted, coherent essay.

2. Topic: Childhood obesity

   Audience: A local organization of parents, youth group leaders, and school officials

   Childhood obesity is a huge problem, you know? There are way too many fat kids in this country, and it's just getting worse. I saw this one kid the other day, and he was like 200 pounds! Everyone knows the problem is getting worse, so what should we do about it? Well, I think we need to get smarter about letting people know how to deal with it and prevent it. Like, we could give better education on healthy eating, and we can have more gym class in school, and we can also have kids checked for family history of fatness. Let's get our country healthy again! We probably can start right with this group!

CHAPTER 9

Graphic organizers for common types of writing

Some students benefit from a visual display of how certain ideas relate to other ideas. Graphic organizers, tools that help students plan their writing by making the relationships between ideas more visually obvious, can be useful for drafting essays and other longer works. The following pages offer graphic organizers for common types of frequently assigned college writing.

✦ 9a A basic essay

An essay is a piece of writing made up of multiple paragraphs on a single subject. Essays can be informative, persuasive, descriptive, narrative, or some combination of these types. You may be used to the five-paragraph essay "formula" from high school, but college instructors don't expect you to be so rigid. Some allow a good deal of experimentation, depending on the topic, your purpose (reason for writing), and your audience (readers).

Sample graphic organizer for a basic essay

These boxes are meant to help you organize your thoughts. They do not necessarily represent individual paragraphs.

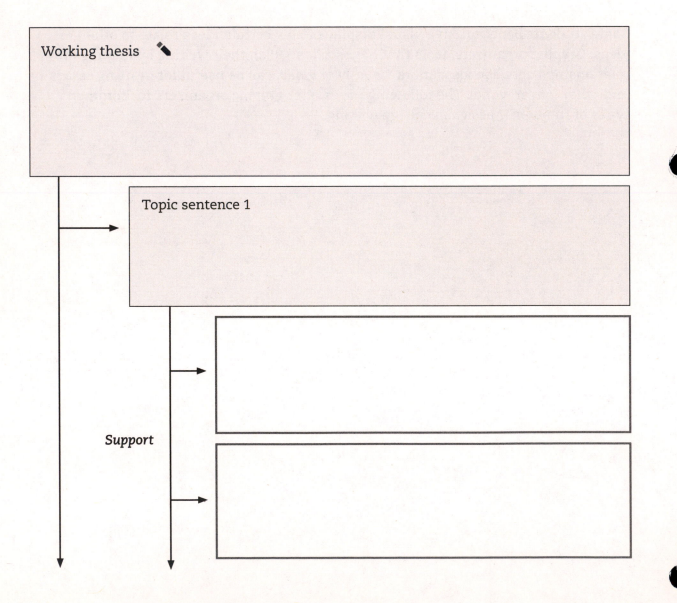

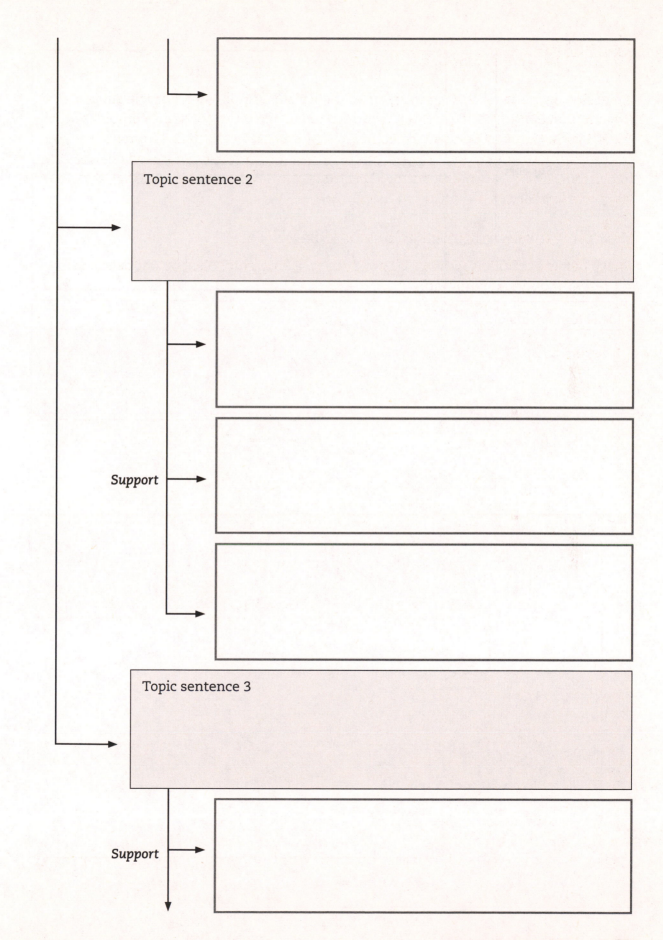

Topic sentence 2

Support

Topic sentence 3

Support

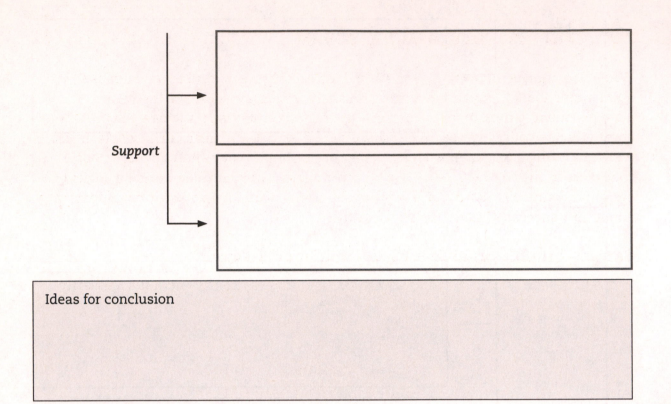

Support

Ideas for conclusion

✦ **9b** An analytical essay

When you analyze something, you break it down to study it, and then you make a judgment about it. If you are writing an analytical essay—about a text, an advertisement, a film, or an art object—your thesis statement is where you communicate your judgment. The rest of the essay looks at parts of the whole. If you were analyzing a magazine advertisement, for example, your analysis might look at the colors in the ad, the typefaces, and the kinds of appeal used (emotional, logical, etc.), and your ideas about those separate elements would help you form a judgment about how successful the ad was.

Sample graphic organizer for an analytical essay

These boxes are meant to help you organize your thoughts. They do not necessarily represent individual paragraphs.

Working thesis ✎

Topic sentence 1

Evidence

Analysis of evidence

Topic sentence 2

Evidence

Analysis of evidence

Topic sentence 3

Evidence

Analysis of evidence

Ideas for conclusion

✦ 9c A compare-and-contrast essay

When you compare two people, places, things, or ideas, you draw your readers' attention to the ways in which the two are similar. When you contrast, you write about the ways in which they are different. Often you will be assigned to do both in the same essay.

There are two basic options for organizing a compare-and-contrast essay. You can focus on important features, comparing the two subjects first on one feature and then, one by one, on the others. Or you can start with all the features of one subject and then look at how the second subject compares on all the same features.

Sample graphic organizer for a compare-and-contrast essay, option 1

These boxes are meant to help you organize your thoughts. They do not necessarily represent individual paragraphs.

Working thesis ✎

First point of comparison

Example from first subject

Example from second subject

Second point of comparison

Example from first subject

Example from second subject

Third point of comparison

Example from first subject

Example from second subject

Ideas for conclusion

Sample graphic organizer for a compare-and-contrast essay, option 2

These boxes are meant to help you organize your thoughts. They do not necessarily represent individual paragraphs.

> **Working thesis**

> **First subject**

> **First point of comparison**

> **Second point of comparison**

> **Third point of comparison**

Second subject

First point of comparison

Second point of comparison

Third point of comparison

Ideas for conclusion

✦ 9d An argument essay

When you write an argument essay, sometimes called a persuasive essay, you set forth a debatable position with evidence; make appeals to emotion (pathos), logic (logos), and/or credibility (ethos); and build common ground. You hope in the end to convince a reader to agree with your position or at least consider it to be a valid position. Argument essays for college courses are almost always written using information from one or more sources.

Where and how you address counterarguments—and thus how you organize your argument essay—will depend on your topic and on your argumentative strategy. You may address counterarguments at the beginning of the essay (see option 1), as you work through individual reasons in support of your own position (see option 2), or at the end of the essay.

Sample graphic organizer for an argument essay, option 1

These boxes are meant to help you organize your thoughts. They do not necessarily represent individual paragraphs.

Working thesis ✎

Problem / background

Opposing position

Your position (reassert thesis)

Evidence

Evidence

Evidence

Ideas for conclusion

Sample graphic organizer for an argument essay, option 2

These boxes are meant to help you organize your thoughts. They do not necessarily represent individual paragraphs.

Working thesis

Problem / background

Reason 1

Evidence and explanation

Counterarguments to Reason 1, if any

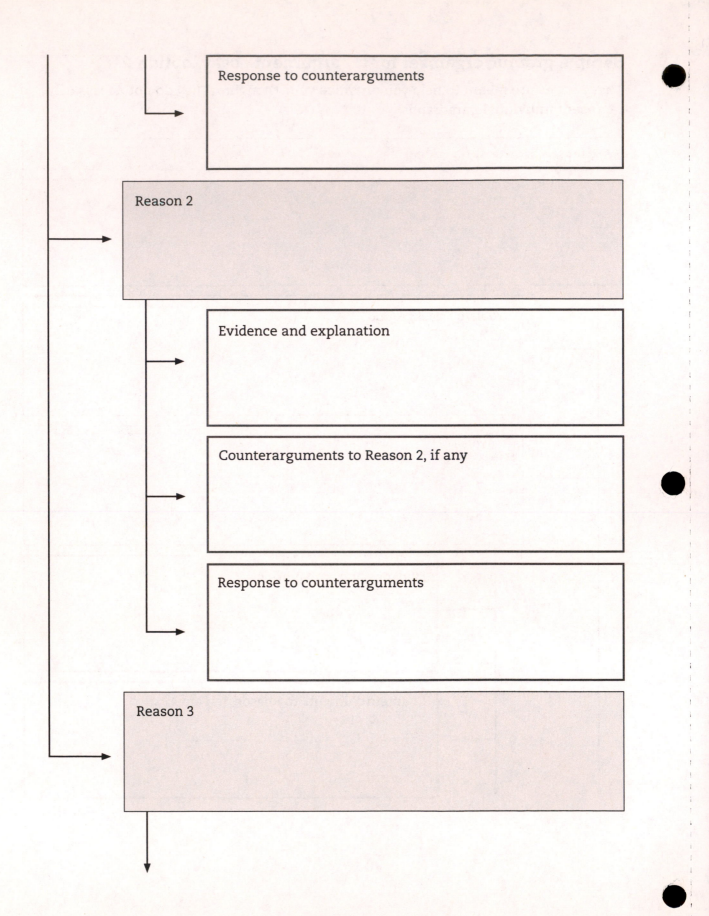

Response to counterarguments

Reason 2

Evidence and explanation

Counterarguments to Reason 2, if any

Response to counterarguments

Reason 3

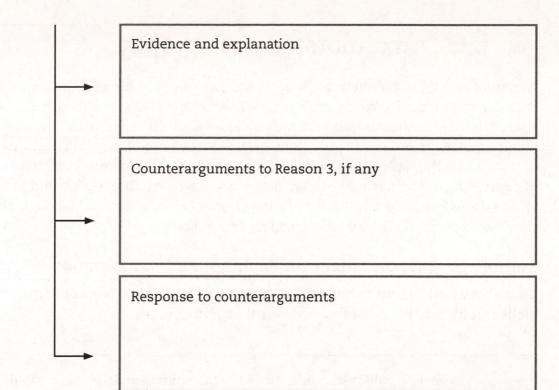

Evidence and explanation

Counterarguments to Reason 3, if any

Response to counterarguments

Ideas for conclusion

✦ 9e An annotated bibliography

An annotated bibliography is a list of sources, arranged in alphabetical order by author, with an accompanying annotation, or brief paragraph (4–7 sentences), describing each source listed. The annotation generally includes a summary of what the source is about and an evaluation, or judgment, of the source's credibility and usefulness. An annotated bibliography gives a researcher an opportunity to demonstrate what kinds of sources he or she has gathered to help answer a research question and to reflect on what role each source might play in a larger project. An annotated bibliography has no thesis statement, no introduction, and no conclusion.

Sample graphic organizer for an annotated bibliography

These boxes are meant to help you organize your thoughts. Your annotated bibliography may include more or fewer than four sources.

> Source 1 (complete publication information in the citation style you are using) ✎

> > Summary
> >
> >
> >
>
> > Evaluation
> >
> >
> >
> >

> Source 2 (complete publication information in the citation style you are using)

Summary

Evaluation

Source 3 (complete publication information in the citation style you are using)

Summary

Evaluation

Source 4 (complete publication information in the citation style you are using)

Summary

Evaluation

✦ **9f** A proposal

A proposal presents a plan and often makes an argument for something. In humanities courses such as composition, proposals are often associated with research projects or other projects. You may be asked to set forth a plan for investigating an idea, solving a problem, or answering a question.

Sample graphic organizer for a proposal

These boxes are meant to help you organize your thoughts. They do not necessarily represent individual paragraphs.

> **Research question** ✎

> **Background**

> **Rationale/so what?**

> **Research conversation**

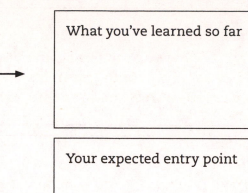

What you've learned so far

Your expected entry point

Search strategy

Traditional/library research

Field research

Project challenges

Anticipated trouble spots

Resources and opportunities

CHAPTER 10

Graphic organizers for common types of paragraphs

For students who benefit from a visual display of how certain ideas relate to other ideas, graphic organizers can be useful for drafting paragraphs as well as essays and other long works. The following pages offer graphic organizers for common types of paragraphs.

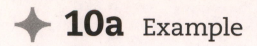 # 10a Example

Examples, perhaps the most common method of development, are appropriate whenever the reader might be tempted to ask, "For example?" A writer who started with a general statement about how director Steven Soderbergh's films demonstrate substantial innovations in storytelling would follow up with a discussion of one or more specific examples of films with new kinds of storytelling.

This template can help you organize your thinking and your notes.

General statement

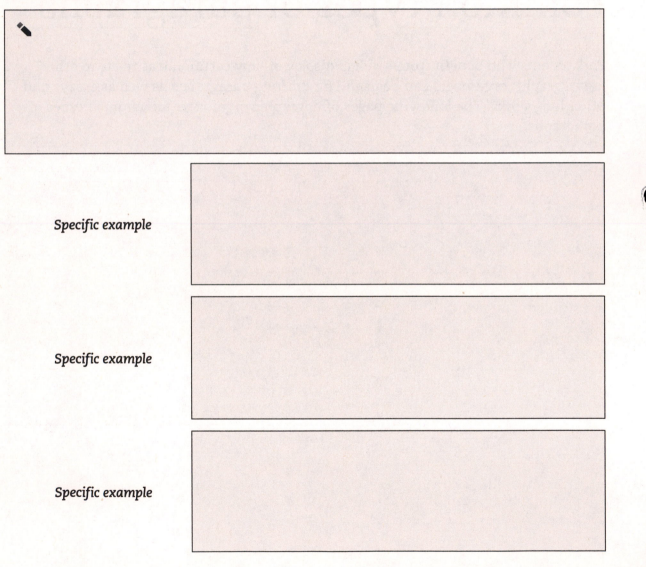

Specific example

Specific example

Specific example

✦ **10b** Illustration

Illustrations are extended examples, frequently presented in story form. When well selected, they can be vivid and effective means of developing a point. A writer who began with a general statement about Harriet Tubman's strategic moves to avoid slave hunters might develop the point with a detailed story of one particular incident in which Tubman successfully avoided capture. The illustration would bring the general statement to life for readers.

This template can help you organize your thinking and your notes.

General statement

Detailed story

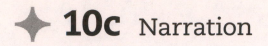 **10c** Narration

A paragraph of narration tells a story or part of a story in the service of a larger argument or other purpose. A writer might, for example, recall her experiences as a biracial child growing up in a predominantly black neighborhood to help her analyze the effects of race relations on children in America.

This template can help you organize your thinking and your notes.

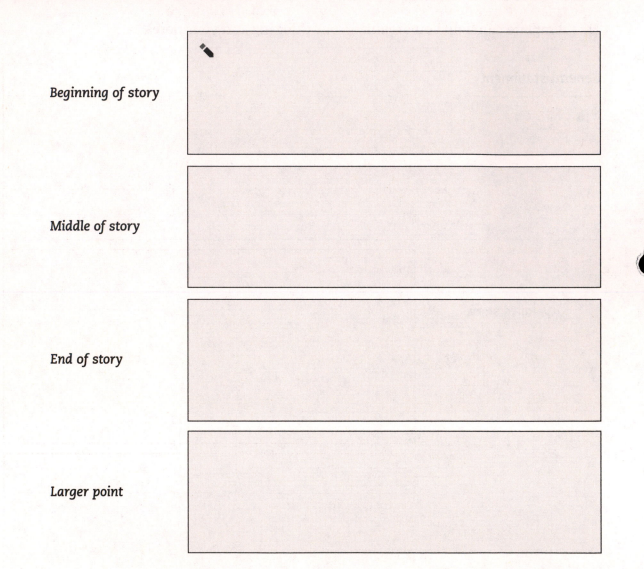

Beginning of story

Middle of story

End of story

Larger point

✦ 10d Description

A descriptive paragraph sketches a portrait of a person, place, or thing using concrete and specific details and vivid language that appeals to one or more of the senses—sight, sound, smell, taste, and touch. A writer describing the aftermath of a devastating hurricane might use phrases such as *once proud and stately homes reduced to snapped and muddy twigs* or *the sopping upholstery smelled like ruin in the air.*

This template can help you organize your thinking and your notes.

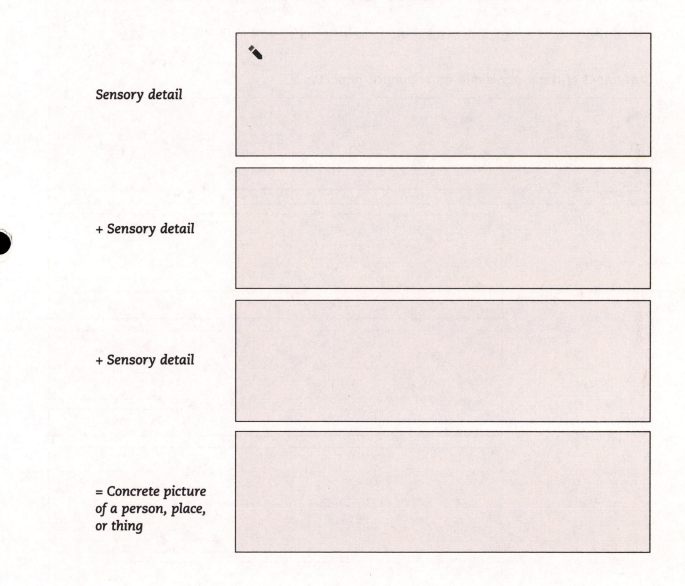

Sensory detail

+ Sensory detail

+ Sensory detail

= Concrete picture of a person, place, or thing

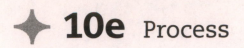 # 10e Process

A process paragraph is structured in chronological order. A writer may choose this pattern either to describe how something is made or done or to explain to readers, step by step, how to do something. To communicate the process to follow in preparing for a job interview, for example, a writer would begin with a statement about what the process is and why it is important or relevant to the audience. Using transition words such as *first*, *then*, *next*, and *finally*, the writer would detail the steps, in order, that the audience would follow to complete the task or understand how to do so.

This template can help you organize your thinking and your notes.

Statement of the process and its relevance/importance

Step

Step

Step

Step

10f Comparison and contrast

To compare two subjects is to draw attention to their similarities, although the word *compare* also has a broader meaning that includes a consideration of differences. To contrast is to focus only on differences. Whether a paragraph stresses similarities or differences, it may be patterned in one of two ways. One approach is to present the two subjects one at a time. A writer who was comparing the leadership styles of two modern heads of state, for example, might present all the qualities of one leader before moving on to all the qualities of the second leader. The other approach is to treat the two subjects together, focusing on one aspect at a time. For example, the writer might present the qualities one by one and compare the two leaders on each quality.

These templates can help you organize your thinking and your notes.

First approach

Statement about how two leaders are similar or different

Person A

One quality

Another quality

A third quality

Person B

One quality

Another quality

A third quality

Second approach

Statement about how two leaders are similar or different

One quality

Person A

Person B

Another quality

Person A

Person B

A third quality

Person A

Person B

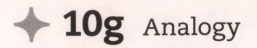

10g Analogy

Analogies draw comparisons between items that appear to have little in common. Writers can use analogies to make something abstract or unfamiliar easier to grasp or to provoke fresh thoughts about a common subject. A writer who was making an argument about the benefits of after-school programs for low-income families might make a comparison between an after-school program and a life raft; another writer might draw a comparison between bumper-to-bumper traffic and a budget approval process for a social program.

This template can help you organize your thinking and your notes.

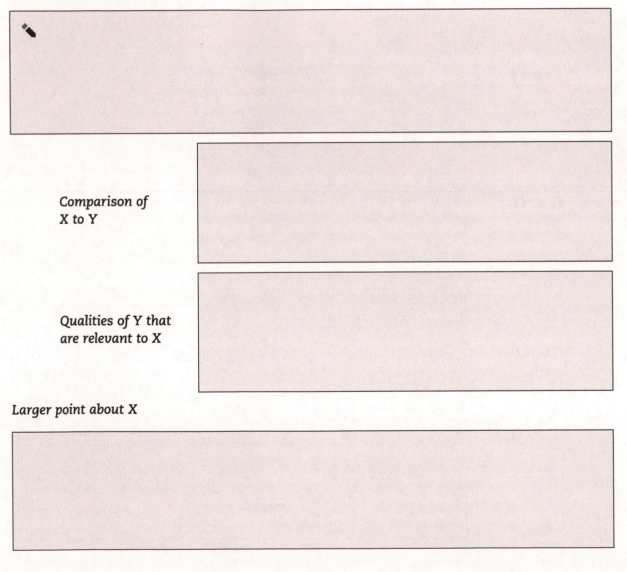

General statement about X

Comparison of X to Y

Qualities of Y that are relevant to X

Larger point about X

✦ **10h** Cause and effect

A paragraph may move from cause to effects or from an effect to its causes. For example, a writer could point out the growing trend toward test-optional college admissions (the effect) and then discuss the factors (the causes) that have led many American colleges and universities to evaluate applicants without using SAT or ACT scores. Or the writer could show how new test-optional policies (the cause) have led to greater racial and economic diversity as well as a broader definition of talent (the effects).

These templates can help you organize your thinking and your notes.

Effect to causes

Effect

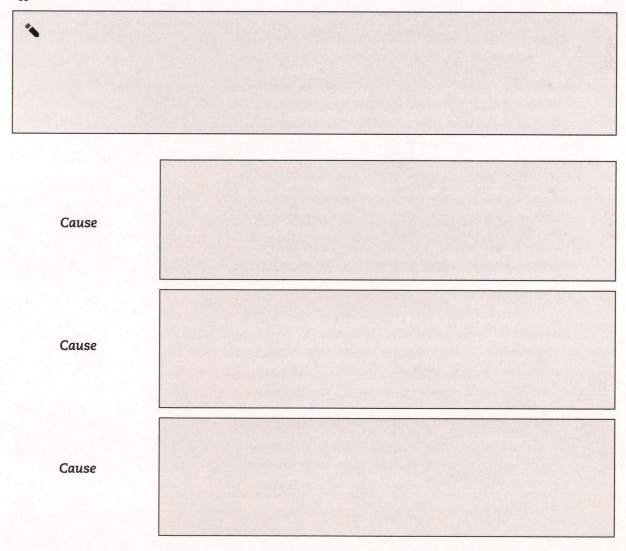

Cause

Cause

Cause

Cause to effects

Cause

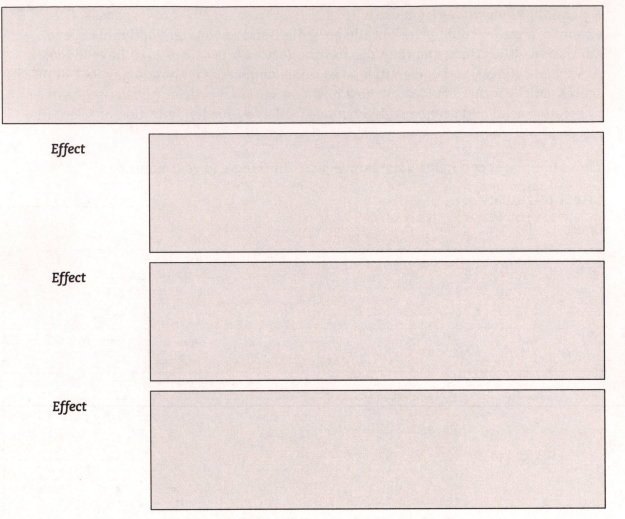

Effect

Effect

Effect

✦ 10i Classification and division

Classification is the grouping of items into categories according to some consistent principle. A writer may wish to classify students who take a gap year (the principle) into three different categories: students who want to earn money to make college more affordable, students who want to travel to build their independence, and students who want to volunteer to make a difference.

These templates can help you organize your thinking and your notes.

Classification

General statement to introduce the principle

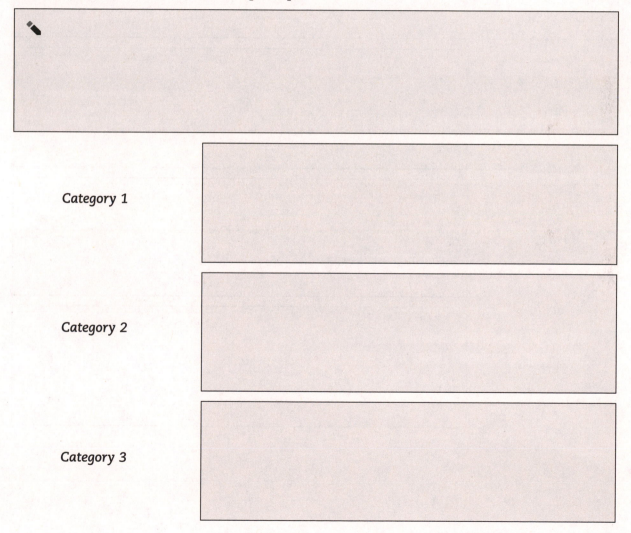

Category 1

Category 2

Category 3

Division takes one item and divides it into parts. Like classification, division should be based on some consistent principle. A writer might, for example, explore what makes a good cover letter for a job application by dividing a typical cover letter into parts (the principle): the opening hook, the qualifications of the applicant, the call to action, and the professional close.

Division

General statement to introduce the whole

Part

Part

Part

✦ **10j** Definition

A definition puts a word or concept into a general class and then provides enough details to distinguish it from others in the same class. For example, if you were reporting on research about where big technology companies get their best ideas, you might define *crowdsourcing* by first placing it in the class of nontraditional business practices and then offering details so that a reader would understand what the practice was and what its chief benefits were.

This template can help you organize your thinking and your notes.

General class

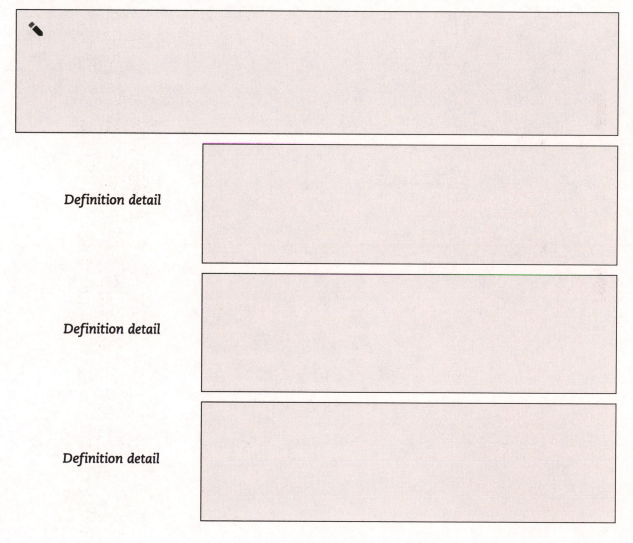

Definition detail

Definition detail

Definition detail

CHAPTER 11

Using sentence guides to develop academic writing skills

Being a college student means being a college writer. No matter what field you are studying, your instructors will ask you to make sense of what you are learning by writing about it. When you work on writing assignments in college, you are, in most cases, writing for an academic audience.

Writing academically means thinking academically—asking a lot of questions, digging into the ideas of others, and entering into scholarly debates and academic conversations. As a college writer, you will be asked to read different kinds of texts; understand and evaluate authors' ideas, arguments, and methods; and contribute your own ideas. In this way, you present yourself as a participant in an academic conversation.

What does it mean to be part of an *academic conversation*? Well, think of it this way: You and your friends may have an ongoing debate about the best film trilogy of all time. During your conversations with one another, you analyze the details of the films, introduce points you want your friends to consider, listen to their ideas, and perhaps cite what the critics have said about a particular trilogy. This kind of conversation is what happens among scholars in academic writing—except that they could be debating the best public policy for a social problem or the most promising new theory in treating disease.

In case you are uncertain about what academic writing *sounds like* or not sure you're any good at it, this chapter offers guidance for you at the sentence level. This chapter helps answer questions such as these:

> How can I present the ideas of others in a way that demonstrates my understanding of the debate?
>
> How can I agree with someone but add a new idea?

How can I disagree with a scholar without seeming, well, rude?

How can I make clear in my writing which ideas are mine and which ideas are someone else's?

The following sections offer sentence guides for you to adapt to your own writing situations. As in all writing that you do, you will have to think about your purpose (reason for writing) and your audience (readers) to decide which guides will be most appropriate for a particular piece of writing or for a certain part of your essay.

The guides are organized to help you present background information, the views and claims of others, and your own views and claims—all in the context of your purpose and audience.

✦ 11a Presenting information and others' views

When you write in academic situations, you may need to spend some time giving background information for or setting a context for your main idea or argument. This often requires you to present or summarize what is known or what has already been said in relation to the question you are asking in your writing.

Presenting what is known or assumed

When you write, you will find that you sometimes need to present something that is known, such as a specific fact or statistic. The following structures are useful when you are providing background information.

> **As we know from history, _____.**
>
> **X has shown that _____.**
>
> **Research by X and Y suggests that _____.**
>
> **According to X, _____ percent of _____ are/favor _____.**

In other situations, you will need to present information that is assumed or that is conventional wisdom.

> **People often believe that _____.**
>
> **Conventional wisdom leads us to believe _____.**
>
> **Many Americans share the idea that _____.**
>
> **_____ is a widely held belief.**

In order to challenge an assumption or a widely held belief, you have to acknowledge it first. Doing so lets your readers see that you are placing your ideas in an appropriate context.

> Although many people are led to believe X, there is significant benefit to considering the merits of Y.

> College students tend to believe that _____ when, in fact, the opposite is much more likely the case.

Presenting others' views

As a writer, you build your own *ethos*, or credibility, by fairly and accurately representing the views of others. As an academic writer, you will be expected to demonstrate your understanding of a text by summarizing the views or arguments of its author(s). To do so, you may use language such as the following.

> X argues that _____.

> X emphasizes the need for _____.

> In this important article, X and Y claim _____.

> X endorses _____ because _____.

> X and Y have recently criticized the idea that _____.

> _____, according to X, is the most critical cause of _____.

Although you will create your own variations of these sentences as you draft and revise, the guides can be useful tools for thinking through how best to present another writer's claim or finding clearly and concisely.

Presenting direct quotations

When the exact words of a source are important for accuracy, authority, emphasis, or flavor, you will want to use a direct quotation. Ordinarily, you will present direct quotations with language of your own that suggests how you are using the source.

> X characterizes the problem this way: ". . ."

> According to X, _____ is defined as ". . ."

> ". . . ," explains X.

> X argues strongly in favor of the policy, pointing out that ". . ."

Note: You will generally cite direct quotations according to the documentation style your readers expect. MLA style, often used in English and other humanities courses, calls for using the author's name paired with a page number, if there is one. APA style, used in most social sciences, requires including the year of publication, generally after the mention of the source, with page numbers after the quoted material. In *Chicago* style, used in history and some humanities courses, superscript numbers (like this[6]) refer readers to footnotes or endnotes. All three styles of in-text citations, like the ones shown below, refer readers to entries in the works cited or reference list.

MLA   Lazarín argues that our overreliance on testing in K-12 schools "does not put students first" (20).

APA   Lazarín (2014) argues that our overreliance on testing in K-12 schools "does not put students first" (p. 20).

Chicago Lazarín argues that our overreliance on testing in K-12 schools "does not put students first."[6]

Many writers use direct quotations to advance an argument of their own:

> **Standardized testing makes it easier for administrators to measure student performance, but it may not be the best way to measure it. Too much testing wears students out and communicates the idea that recall is the most important skill we want them to develop. Even education policy advisor Melissa Lazarín argues that our overreliance on testing in K-12 schools "does not put students first" (20).**

Student writer's idea

Source's idea

Presenting alternative views

Most debates, whether they are scholarly or popular, are complex, as there are often more than two sides to an issue. Sometimes you will have to synthesize the views of multiple participants in the debate before you introduce your own ideas.

> **On the one hand, X reports that _____, but on the other hand, Y insists that _____.**
>
> **Even though X endorses the policy, Y refers to it as ". . ."**
>
> **X, however, isn't convinced and instead argues _____.**
>
> **X and Y have supported the theory in the past, but new research by Z suggests that _____.**

✦ 11b Presenting your own views

When you write for an academic audience, you have to demonstrate that you are familiar with the views of others who are asking the same kinds of questions as you are. Much of the academic writing that you will be assigned will require you to put your arguments in the context of existing arguments—in a way asking you to connect the known to the new.

When you are asked to write a summary or an informative text, your own views and arguments are generally not called for. However, much of the writing you will be assigned to do in college will call for you to take a persuasive stance and present a reasoned argument—at times in response to a single text, and at other times in response to multiple texts.

Presenting your own views: Agreement and extension

Sometimes you agree with the author of a source.

> X's argument is convincing because _____.
>
> Because X's approach is so _____, it is the best way to _____.
>
> X makes an important point when she says _____.

Other times you find you agree with the author of a source, but you want to extend the point or go a bit deeper with your own investigation. You want to acknowledge the source for getting you so far in the conversation, but then move the conversation along with a related comment or finding.

> X's proposal for _____ is indeed worth considering. Going one step further, _____.
>
> X makes the claim that _____. By extension, isn't it also true, then, that _____?
>
> _____ has been adequately explained by X. Now, let's move beyond that idea and ask whether _____.

Presenting your own views: Queries and skepticism

You may be intimidated when you're asked to talk back to a source, especially if the source is a well-known scholar or expert or even just a frequent voice in a particular debate. College-level writing requires you to be skeptical, however, and approach academic questions with the mind of an investigator. It is OK to doubt, to question, to challenge—because the end result is often new knowledge or new understanding about a subject.

> Couldn't it also be argued that _____?
>
> But is everyone willing to agree that this is the case?
>
> While X insists that _____ is so, he is perhaps asking the wrong question to begin with.
>
> The claims that X and Y have made, while intelligent and well-meaning, leave many unconvinced because they have failed to consider _____.

Presenting your own views: Disagreement or correction

You may find that at times the only response you have to a text or to an author is complete disagreement.

> X's claims about _____ are completely misguided.

> X presents a long metaphor comparing _____ to _____; in the end, the comparison is unconvincing because _____.

It can be tempting to disregard a source completely if you detect a piece of information that strikes you as false or that you know to be untrue. But it's often a better idea to make clear how or why the information is false.

> Although X reports that _____, recent studies indicate that this is not the case.

> While X and Y insist that _____ is so, an examination of their figures shows that thay have made an important miscalculation.

A note about using "I"

Some disciplines look favorably on the use of the first-person "I" in academic writing. Others do not, instead recommending that you stick to using the third person. When you are given a writing assignment, either ask your instructor for guidance or look at sample texts he or she has given you.

First person (I, *me, my, we, us, our*)

I question Heddinger's methods and small sample size.

Harnessing children's technology obsession in the classroom is, I believe, the key to improving learning.

Lanza's interpretation focuses on circle imagery as symbolic of the family; my analysis leads me in a different direction entirely.

We would, in fact, benefit from looser laws about farming on our personal property.

Third person (names and other nouns)

Heddinger's methods and small sample size are questionable.

Harnessing children's technology obsession in the classroom is the key to improving learning.

Lanza's interpretation focuses on circle imagery as symbolic of the family; other readers' analyses point in a different direction entirely.

Many Americans would, in fact, benefit from looser laws about farming on personal property.

You may think that not being able to use "I" in an essay in which you present your ideas about a topic is unfair or will lead to weaker statements. But you can make a strong argument even when you write in the third person. Third-person writing allows you to sound more assertive, credible, and academic.

Presenting and countering objections to your argument

Effective college writers know that their arguments are stronger when they anticipate objections that others might raise.

> **Some will object to this proposal on the grounds that** _____.
>
> **Not everyone will embrace** _____; **they may argue instead that** _____.

Countering, or responding to, opposing voices fairly and respectfully strengthens your writing and your *ethos*, or credibility.

> **X and Y might contend that this interpretation is faulty; however,** _____.
>
> **Most** _____ **believe that there is too much risk in this approach. But what they have failed to take into consideration is** _____.

✦ 11c Persuading by putting it all together

Readers of academic writing often want to know what's at stake in a particular debate or text. They want to know why they should care and why they should keep reading. In addition to crafting individual sentences, you must, of course, keep the bigger picture in mind as you attempt to persuade, inform, evaluate, or review.

Presenting stakeholders

When you write, you may be doing so as a member of a group affected by the research conversation you have entered. For example, you may be among the thousands of students in your state whose level of debt could change as a result of new laws about financing a college education. In this case, you are a *stakeholder* in the matter. In other words, you have a direct interest in the matter, as a person who could be affected by the outcome of the debate. On the other hand, you may be writing as an investigator of a topic that interests you but that you aren't directly connected with. You may be trying to persuade your audience on behalf of a group of interested stakeholders of which you yourself are not a member.

You can give your writing some teeth if you make clear who is affected by the issue and the decisions that have been or will be made about it. The groups of stakeholders are highlighted in the following sentences.

Viewers of Kurosawa's films may not agree with X that _____.

The research will come as a surprise to parents of children with Type 1 diabetes.

X's claims have the power to offend potentially every low-wage earner in the state.

Marathoners might want to reconsider their training regimen if stories such as those told by X and Y are validated by the medical community.

Presenting the "so what"

For readers to be motivated to read your writing, they have to believe that you're addressing something that matters to them, something that matters very much to you, or something that should matter to us all. Good academic writing often hooks readers with a sense of urgency—a serious response to a reader's "So what?"

Having a frank discussion about _____ now will put us in a far better position to deal with _____ in the future. If we are unwilling or unable to do so, we risk _____.

Such a breakthrough will affect _____ in three significant ways.

It is easy to believe that the stakes aren't high enough to be alarming; in fact, _____ will be affected by _____.

Widespread disapproval of and censorship of such fiction/films/art will mean _____ for us in the future. Culture should represent _____.

New experimentation in _____ could allow scientists to investigate _____ in ways they couldn't have imagined _____ years ago.

Presenting the players and positions in a debate

Some disciplines ask writers to compose a review of the literature as part of a larger project—or sometimes as a free-standing assignment. In a review of the literature, the writer sets forth a research question, summarizes the key sources that have addressed the question, puts the current research in the context of other voices in the research conversation, and identifies any gaps in the research.

Writing that presents a debate, its players, and their positions can often be lengthy. What follows, however, will give you the sense of the flow of ideas and turns in such a piece of writing.

_____ affects more than 30% of children in America, and signs point to a worsening situation in years to come because of A, B, and C. Solutions to the problem have eluded even the sharpest policy minds and brightest researchers. In an important 2003 study, W found that _____, which pointed to more problems than solutions. [. . .] Research by X and Y made strides in our understanding of _____ but still didn't offer specific strategies for children and families struggling to _____. [. . .] When Z rejected both the methods and the findings of X and Y, arguing that _____, policymakers and health care experts were optimistic. [. . .] Too much discussion of _____, however, and too little discussion of _____ may lead us to solutions that are ultimately too expensive to sustain.

Student writer states the problem.

Student writer summarizes the views of others on the topic.

Student writer presents her view in the context of current research.

Verbs matter

Using a variety of verbs in your sentences can add strength and clarity as you present others' views and your own views.

When you want to present a view neutrally		
acknowledges	observes	
adds	points out	
admits	reports	
comments	suggests	
contends	writes	
notes		

X points out that the plan had unintended outcomes.

When you want to present a stronger view		
argues	emphasizes	
asserts	insists	
declares		

Y argues in favor of a ban on _____; but Z insists the plan is misguided.

When you want to show agreement	agrees
	confirms
	endorses
	An **endorsement** of X's position is smart for a number of reasons.

When you want to show contrast or disagreement	compares
	denies
	disputes
	refutes
	rejects
	The town must come together and reject X's claims that _____ is in the best interest of the citizens.

When you want to anticipate an objection	admits
	acknowledges
	concedes
	Y admits that closer study of _____, with a much larger sample size, is necessary for _____.

CHAPTER 12

Integrating sources: Quotation sandwiching (MLA style)

College writing assignments often call for you to read or view sources such as articles, reports, fact sheets, or TED talks and then use those sources as evidence in your own writing. Some sources will provide background information, others will offer data and statistics, and still others will make arguments for or counterarguments to your position.

One challenge in writing with sources is figuring out how to blend your ideas and the ideas of others smoothly. Chapter 11 provides sentence guides, giving you a sentence-level method for developing this kind of academic skill. This chapter offers a method for developing paragraphs in which you balance your ideas and the ideas in a source to move your argument forward. This method, which involves sandwiching source material between sentences of your own, is intended to help you show your readers how the source information relates to your claim or argument. By creating a context for your source material rather than just dropping it in, you can prepare your readers, which is much better than catching them unaware.

✦ **12a** Integrating a single source

The following grid shows how one writer began to assemble a paragraph in which he discusses, as part of a larger essay on changes in digital culture, how social media can make people feel more lonely. The shaded part of the grid is the "meat"—the source material that helps the writer to make his argument.

Claim Your topic sentence for this paragraph	It is surprising that with so many more ways to connect with others, more Americans than ever report feeling lonely.
Meaningful half-sentence (signal phrase) to introduce quotation Author's name, title, summary of the evidence	In an article called "The Cure for Disconnection," journalist Jennifer Latson lays part of the blame on our digital culture and
Argument verb *suggests* *contends* *argues* *affirms* *demonstrates* *insists* *reveals* *emphasizes*	argues
Quotation/evidence Direct quotation from text, using ellipsis (…) or brackets [to change words or word endings] as needed	that "[c]onversations by text or Facebook messenger may be filled with smile emojis, but they leave us feeling empty because they lack depth"
Citation and period (Author's last name and page number) OR ("Abbreviated Title" and page number). If you mentioned the author or title earlier, you don't need it in the parentheses. If the source is a web source without pages, you don't need a page number.	(49).
Explanation or paraphrase *Basically, X is saying that . . .* *In other words, X argues that . . .* *X suggests that . . .* *X's point is that . . .* *To put it another way, . . .*	To put it another way, Latson suggests that we don't seem to feel satisfied by the interactions we have on social media platforms; this way of talking with others still ends up feeling impersonal.

Interpretation, significance	Although the problem of digitally induced loneliness might seem to affect mostly teens and young adults, more people of every age are having fewer face-to-face interactions, and the consequences could be significant.
This demonstrates that . . .	
This idea is important because . . .	
Ultimately, what is at stake here is . . .	
Although X may seem of concern to only a small group of _____, it should in fact concern anyone who cares about . . .	
And so, we should . . .	

Putting together such a grid can be a useful exercise; when you have your ideas and your source information laid out this way, assembling a paragraph can be much easier. See the following draft paragraph.

SAMPLE COMPLETED PARAGRAPH WITH QUOTATION SANDWICH

It is surprising that with so many more ways to connect with others, more Americans than ever report feeling lonely. [*You may want to include more of your own writing after your topic sentence and before the quotation. That information goes here.*] In an article called "The Cure for Disconnection," journalist Jennifer Latson lays part of the blame on our digital culture and argues that "[c]onversations by text or Facebook messenger may be filled with smile emojis, but they leave us feeling empty because they lack depth" (49). To put it another way, Latson suggests that we don't seem to feel satisfied by the interactions we have on social media platforms; this way of talking with others still ends up feeling impersonal. Although the problem of digitally induced loneliness might seem to affect mostly teens and young adults, more people of every age are having fewer face-to-face interactions, and the consequences could be important.

Try making your own quotation sandwich by providing context before and interpretation after a source that you've chosen to use in your writing. Here's a blank grid. Keep in mind that the grid is intended to be a flexible guide. You may choose to make adaptations based on your sources and your purpose.

Claim Your topic sentence for this paragraph	✎
Meaningful half-sentence (signal phrase) to introduce quotation Author's name, title, summary of the evidence	
Argument verb *suggests* *contends* *argues* *affirms* *demonstrates* *insists* *reveals* *emphasizes*	
Quotation/evidence Direct quotation from text, using ellipsis (. . .) or brackets [ ] as needed to alter the quotation responsibly	
Citation and period (Author's last name and page number) OR ("Abbreviated Title" and page number). If you mentioned the author or title earlier, you don't need it in the parentheses. If the source is a web source without pages, you don't need a page number.	
Explanation or paraphrase *Basically, X is saying that . . .* *In other words, X argues that . . .* *X suggests that . . .* *X's point is that . . .* *To put it another way, . . .*	
Interpretation, significance *This demonstrates that . . .* *This idea is important because . . .* *Ultimately, what is at stake here is . . .* *Although X may seem of concern to only a small group of _____, it should in fact concern anyone who cares about . . .* *And so, we should . . .*	

✦ 12b Integrating more than one source (synthesizing)

Often you will find yourself using more than one source to help you make a single point or to help you advance a part of your argument. This is what happens in most research writing, for it reflects the conversation that is happening about the topic. As the writer, you will be in that conversation, and you will weave in sources as you need them. In other words, you will synthesize multiple sources and show how the ideas in those sources relate to one another and to your ideas.

The following grid shows you one writer's notes for a paragraph in which he synthesizes multiple sources in the service of his own argument. Using the sandwich metaphor, you can consider this kind of paragraph a "club sandwich" with several layers. The shaded part of the grid is the "meat"—the source material that helps the writer to make his argument.

Claim Your topic sentence for this paragraph	**It is surprising that with so many more ways to connect with others, more Americans than ever report feeling lonely.**
Meaningful half-sentence (signal phrase) to introduce quotation Author's name, title, summary of the evidence	**In an article called "The Cure for Disconnection," journalist Jennifer Latson lays part of the blame on our digital culture and**
Argument verb *suggests* *contends* *argues* *affirms* *demonstrates* *insists* *reveals* *emphasizes* *maintains*	**argues**
Quotation/evidence Direct quotation from text, using ellipsis (. . .) or brackets [ ] as needed to alter the quotation responsibly	**that "[c]onversations by text or Facebook messenger may be filled with smile emojis, but they leave us feeling empty because they lack depth"**

Citation and period (Author's last name and page number) OR ("Abbreviated Title" and page number). If you mentioned the author or title earlier, you don't need it in the parentheses. If the source is a web source without pages, you don't need a page number.	(49).
Transition to next evidence Signal phrase or half-sentence to link to a quotation from another piece that deepens, clarifies, builds on, or reverses the first evidence	University of Chicago psychology professor John T. Cacioppo has found that people of all ages, however, deny their own feelings, but he
Argument verb *suggests* *contends* *argues* *affirms* *demonstrates* *insists* *reveals* *emphasizes* *maintains*	contends
Quotation/evidence Direct quotation from text, using ellipsis (. . .) or brackets [ ] as needed to alter the quotation responsibly	that "[d]enying you feel lonely makes no more sense than denying you feel hunger." He describes loneliness as an "aversive signal much like thirst, hunger, or pain"
Citation and period (Author's last name and page number) OR ("Abbreviated Title" and page number). If the source is quoted in another source, use "qtd. in." If the source is a web source without pages, you don't need a page number.	(qtd. in Hafner).
Interpretation/significance *This demonstrates that . . .* *This idea is important because . . .* *Ultimately, what is at stake here is . . .* *Although X may seem of concern to only a small group of _____, it should in fact concern anyone who cares about . . .* *And so, we should . . .*	These ideas point to an important development in our psychological health. Our digital culture leads us to believe we have it all—and all a click away. But the emptiness that these researchers point to signals a need for something more personal and meaningful.

## Short sentence or question for impact Short sentence to reaffirm your thesis, move your idea along, and break up the long paragraph—for example, *But that's not enough.* *We deserve more.* *What can we do about it?* *Where does this leave us?*	**So what can we do?**
## Transition to next evidence Third meaningful half-sentence to link to a quotation from another piece that deepens, clarifies, refines, or reverses the second evidence	**It may sound cliché, but Latner**
## Argument verb *suggests* *contends* *argues* *affirms* *demonstrates* *insists* *reveals* *emphasizes* *maintains*	**maintains**
## Quotation/evidence Direct quotation from text or a paraphrase or summary of the source's idea, which still needs a citation	**that the most basic thing we can do is to create situations that allow us to be our "authentic self with another person," which can mean practicing by getting together regularly with one or more people without our smartphones for an hour at a time**
## Citation and period	**(50).**
## Reaction to evidence Analysis of the evidence—what this quotation demonstrates, reveals, or suggests *X's suggestion is . . .* *This quotation reveals . . .* *This evidence demonstrates . . .*	**Latner's suggestion is a good one. Most people feel more satisfied after a substantial one-on-one conversation than they do after posting a fleeting thought and getting twenty "likes." We need the push-and-pull of ideas, eye contact, tone of voice, and other things that make us human.**

Reaffirmation of link to thesis How all of this reinforces and advances your argument	Although the problem of digitally induced loneliness might seem to affect mostly teens and young adults, more people of every age are having fewer face-to-face interactions, and the consequences could be significant.

The following assembled sample paragraph shows a balance of sources (highlighted) and original words of the student writer.

SAMPLE COMPLETED PARAGRAPH IN "CLUB SANDWICH" STYLE (SYNTHESIS)

It is surprising that with so many more ways to connect with others, more Americans than ever report feeling lonely. In an article called "The Cure for Disconnection," journalist Jennifer Latson lays part of the blame on our digital culture and argues that "[c]onversations by text or Facebook messenger may be filled with smile emojis, but they leave us feeling empty because they lack depth" (49). University of Chicago psychology professor John T. Cacioppo has found that people of all ages, however, deny their own feelings, but he contends that "[d]enying you feel lonely makes no more sense than denying you feel hunger." He describes loneliness as an "aversive signal much like thirst, hunger, or pain" (qtd. in Hafner). These ideas point to an important development in our psychological health. Our digital culture leads us to believe we have it all—and all a click away. But the emptiness that these researchers point to signals a need for something more personal and meaningful. So what can we do? It may sound cliché, but Latner maintains that the most basic thing we can do is to create situations that allow us to be our "authentic self with another person," which can mean practicing by getting together regularly with one or more people without our smartphones for an hour at a time (50). Latner's suggestion is a good one. Most people feel more satisfied after a substantial one-on-one conversation than they do after posting a fleeting thought and getting twenty "likes." We need the push-and-pull of ideas, eye contact, tone of voice, and other things that make us human. Although the problem of digitally induced loneliness might seem to affect mostly teens and young adults, more people of every age are having fewer face-to-face interactions, and the consequences could be significant.

You can use the following blank grid to assemble your own synthesis paragraph, making adjustments as needed for your sources and your purpose.

Claim Your topic sentence for this paragraph	✎
Meaningful half-sentence (signal phrase) to introduce quotation Author's name, title, summary of the evidence	
Argument verb *suggests* *contends* *argues* *affirms* *demonstrates* *insists* *reveals* *emphasizes* *maintains*	
Quotation/evidence Direct quotation from text, using ellipsis (. . .) or brackets [ ] as needed to alter the quotation responsibly	
Citation and period (Author's last name and page number) OR ("Abbreviated Title" and page number). If you mention the author or title earlier, you don't need it in the parentheses. If the source is a web source without pages, you don't need a page number.	
Transition to next evidence Signal phrase or half-sentence to link to a quotation from another piece that deepens, clarifies, builds on, or reverses the first evidence	
Argument verb *suggests* *contends* *argues* *affirms* *demonstrates* *insists* *reveals* *emphasizes* *maintains*	

Quotation/evidence Direct quotation from text, using ellipsis (. . .) or brackets [ ] as needed to alter the quotation responsibly	
Citation and period (Author's last name and page number) OR ("Abbreviated Title" and page number). If the source is quoted in another source, use "qtd. in." If the source is a web source without pages, you don't need a page number.	
Interpretation, significance *This demonstrates that . . .* *This idea is important because . . .* *Ultimately, what is at stake here is . . .* *Although X may seem of concern to only a small group of _____, it should in fact concern anyone who cares about . . .* *And so, we should . . .*	
Short sentence or question for impact Short sentence to reaffirm your thesis, move your idea along, and break up the long paragraph—for example, *But that's not enough.* *We deserve more.* *What can we do about it?* *Where does this leave us?*	
Transition to next evidence Third meaningful half-sentence to link to a quotation from another piece that deepens, clarifies, refines, or reverses the second evidence	

Argument verb *suggests* *contends* *argues* *affirms* *demonstrates* *insists* *reveals* *emphasizes* *maintains*	
Quotation/evidence Direct quotation from text or a paraphrase or summary of the source's idea, which still needs a citation	
Citation and period	
Reaction to evidence Analysis of evidence—what this quotation demonstrates, reveals, or suggests *X's suggestion is…* *This quotation reveals…* *This evidence demonstrates…*	
Reaffirmation of link to thesis How all of this reinforces and advances your argument	

CHAPTER 13

Revising paragraphs and essays

For experienced writers, revising is rarely a one-step process. As you gain experience with college writing, you will learn to give your attention to the larger, more global elements of your writing first—the focus, organization, content, and overall strategy. You can make improvements in sentence structure, word choice, grammar, and punctuation later. It doesn't make any sense to puzzle over sentences that you may not keep from draft to draft.

For example, it might be tempting to "fix" some of the problems in this sample opening paragraph of an essay about the advantages of watching athletic events at home instead of in person. But before you spend time on spelling, capitalization, and punctuation, you might want to ask a few bigger questions:

✧ What is the main argument?

✧ Is it clear to the reader where an essay with this introduction is headed?

Sports on TV—A Win or a Loss

Team sports are a big part of american life and they have a tendency to bring people together. They require that team members cooperate with one another to fulfill the game plan, they also create shared enthusiasm among fans. Thanks to HD TV and innovative camera work, this togetherness seems available to almost everyone and we can all feel part of the game. Some fans get out of hand and take wins and losses too seriously whether at the staduim or on their couch. We do not have to buy tickets or travel to a stadium to see the World Series or the Super Bowl, these games are on television, we can enjoy them from the comfort of our own living room. In the past 20 years the percent of people who say they'd rather attend a game in person has dropped from 54% to 29% (Rovell). Its more affordable and enjoyable.

In your own words, identify what you see as some of the bigger, more global problems in this sample opening paragraph. ✎ _____

_____

_____

_____

_____

✦ 13a Tips for revising globally

The following tips for making global revisions may help when you revise your own writing.

- ✧ Reread the assignment rubric or your instructor's expectations.

- ✧ Approach global revision in cycles.

- ✧ Seek feedback from reviewers, tutors, or other readers.

Reread the assignment rubric or your instructor's expectations.
Your instructor probably gave you a hard copy or posted a digital copy of the assignment sheet, which likely described the purpose, audience, type of writing expected, length, and any notes about the process for the assignment. Read the assignment sheet again before tackling your revision. If your teacher distributed a detailed list of grading criteria, have that handy as you revise. If one of the criteria is that the essay must include "a thesis statement that is debatable and sets forth your position," you will want to question, as part of your revision process, whether a reader could agree or disagree with your thesis.

Approach global revision in cycles.
Global revision can be complex and time-consuming, so it's best to approach it in multiple passes or cycles. Leave yourself a whole day or evening to revise—accept that you can't revise anything in a half hour. Make a separate pass through your draft for each of these goals:

- ✧ **Sharpen the focus.** Look for opportunities to clarify the introduction and the thesis and to delete any text that is off the point or that doesn't help you achieve your purpose.

- ✧ **Improve the organization.** Look for opportunities to add or sharpen topic sentences, move blocks of text, or break ideas into separate paragraphs.

❖ **Strengthen the content.** Consider where you might add specific facts, details, and examples. Look for opportunities to emphasize major ideas.

❖ **Clarify the point of view.** Make the point of view appropriate for your purpose and consistent throughout your piece.

❖ **Engage the audience.** Look for opportunities to motivate readers to read on, to adjust the tone, or to change your appeals.

Seek feedback from reviewers, tutors, or other readers.

Many of us resist global revision because we find it difficult to distance ourselves from a draft. We tend to review our work from our own perspective, not our audience's. Put your draft aside for a day or two, and then enlist the help of one or more reviewers such as classmates, family members, friends, a writing center tutor, or your instructor. Remind them that you are focusing on bigger issues and will later turn to sentence-level mistakes.

ACTIVITY ✦ What revision goals would you suggest to the writer of the following brief essay? Remember to focus on global issues.

When people find out our family has moved seven times, they say some version of, "Oh you poor thing!" or roll their eyes. I just smile.

Our house is not crowded with furniture, and none of us have a lot of unnecessary objects. A lot of people my age have the clothes they wore in middle school still, but not me. I also don't really have my toys or books from childhood. Because we have moved so often, I have learned to acquire and save fewer things. Children in military families are used to packing and packing light.

We have been taught by our moves to become active in our church whenever we can. Meeting people is hard but we can generally count on finding friends at the church—even in church youth groups and young adult leadership groups. I have not kept all of the projects I have made over the years in Sunday school.

I like to sing, so I usually try to take part in the choir, and I have made several friends that way.

My brother and sister and I have grown close. With every move we knew that even if we didn't find friends we could count on each other. We would spend many nights playing hide and seek or board games or in recent years video games together. We have a lot of shared experiences with these moves and a lot of funny jokes that only our family knows. For example, my mom loves to bake but she usally burns something, like cookies, every time she's getting used to a new stove. A plate of burned cookies usually begins a family ceremony to celebrate yet another successful move.

Problems with the draft (write them here or mark up the draft):

✎ _____

_____

_____

Suggestions you would make:

_____

_____

_____

_____

✦ **13b** Tips for revising sentences

When you revise sentences, you focus on strength and effectiveness. When you edit, you check for correctness. Both are needed—but only after the main ideas, evidence, and organization are in place. Sentence revision, like global revision, may be approached in cycles. The main purposes for revising sentences are to strengthen, clarify, vary, and correct them.

Experiment with how to make revisions and corrections. Some writers do so on screen; others print a hard copy, make changes, and then go back to the document on screen.

✧ **Strengthen sentences.** Look for opportunities to use more active verbs, to delete extra words, and to choose language more appropriate for your subject and audience. (Check your handbook for active verbs, wordy sentences, and appropriate language.)

✧ **Clarify sentences.** Think about where you can balance parallel ideas, untangle awkward or mixed constructions, or replace vague pronouns. (Check your handbook for parallelism, mixed constructions, and pronoun reference.)

✧ **Vary sentences.** Look for opportunities to combine choppy sentences, break up long sentences, and choose different sentence patterns to vary sentence openings. (Check your handbook for variety, emphasis, coordination, and subordination.)

✧ **Correct sentences.** Pay attention to the verbs you use, the sentence boundaries you create, and the punctuation you use. (Check your handbook for subject-verb agreement, fragments, run-ons, commas, and apostrophes.)

Note: Grammar checkers and spell checkers can be useful tools; depending on them to catch every mistake or weak sentence is unwise, however. If you are not confident in your proofreading skills, ask a friend or tutor to point out some patterns or problem areas.

ACTIVITY ✦ What sentence-level revisions would you suggest to the following paragraph from an essay that analyzes the song "Pumped Up Kicks" by Foster the People? You can edit directly below.

The lyrics tells us about a boy a "kid" whose "Daddy works a long day." He spends his day unsupervised Robert is alone in his house and all by himself and his free time is spent digging in "his dad's closet" trying to find cigarettes. There's not really a hint of any kind of relationship. At least a positive relationship. The father comes "home late" and Robert is left waiting "for a long time." Even if we can't relate to Robert. Maybe we can understand his actions threatening gun violence in his school could possibly be the result of an unloving home. Robert is a sympathetic character.

Pay particular attention to the comments you receive on drafts turned in during the first several weeks of class. If you find you are getting similar comments draft after draft, a pattern may be emerging and you can focus your changes. Keeping an editing log may help. In an editing log, you record frequent mistakes and note the places in your handbook where you can find help.

CHAPTER 14

Reading exercises

Exercise 14-a
Using titles as on-ramps for reading

Name	
Date	Section

To read about this topic, see the section on on-ramps for active strategic reading in chapter 5 of this workbook.

For each of the following titles, describe what you expect to read about and why. What can you tell about the author's purpose, audience, or approach from the title?

1. "Super Daddy Issues: Parental Figures, Masculinity, and Superhero Films"

   _____

   _____

   _____

   _____

2. "The Media Impact of Animal Disease on US Meat Demand"

   _____

   _____

   _____

   _____

3. "Student Nonsuicidal Self-injury: A Protocol for School Counselors"

   _____

   _____

   _____

   _____

Exercise 14-b
Using patterns of organization as on-ramps for reading

To read about this topic, see the section on on-ramps for active strategic reading in chapter 5 of this workbook.

For each of the following passages, select the pattern of organization from the choices given, and then explain what clues led you to make that selection. How does knowing the pattern help you figure out the logic of what you are reading?

1. Is this paragraph organized by narration (telling a story), illustration (general statement followed by examples), or process (showing how to do something)?

> As they confronted this devastating crime wave, black officials exhibited a complicated and sometimes overlapping mix of impulses. Some displayed tremendous hostility toward perpetrators of crime, describing them as a "cancer" that had to be cut away from the rest of the black community. Others pushed for harsher penalties but acknowledged that these measures would not solve the crisis at hand. Some even expressed sympathy for the plight of criminal defendants, who they knew were disproportionately black. But that sympathy was rarely sufficient to overcome the claims of black crime victims, who often argued that a punitive approach was necessary to protect that African-American community—including many of its most impoverished members—from the ravages of crime.

Source: Forman, James Jr. *Locking Up Our Own: Crime and Punishment in Black America.* Farrar, Straus and Giroux, 2017, pp. 10–11.

_____

_____

_____

_____

_____

_____

_____

2. Is this paragraph organized by definition (telling the meaning of a word or concept), cause and effect (explaining the results of or reason for an event), or comparison and contrast (showing how two things are similar and different)?

Let us begin with the critical differences between the missions and philosophies of the two federal agencies involved in regulating dietary supplements, the Food and Drug Administration (FDA) and the Federal Trade Commission (FTC). The FDA's mandate is to promote *safety*: its job is to ensure that conventional foods, dietary supplements, and drugs are safe and labeled accurately, and that drugs do something useful according to science-based standards—in other words, as verified by clinical trials. The FTC has a decidedly different mission: to promote *business competition*. One way it does so is by preventing unfair commercial practices such as false advertising. Thus both agencies are involved in regulating certain actions of supplement companies.

Source: Nestle, Marion. *Food Politics: How the Food Industry Influences Nutrition and Health.* University of California Press, 2013, p. 227.

_____

_____

_____

_____

_____

_____

_____

_____

Exercise 14-c
Using vocabulary as an on-ramp for reading

To read about this topic, see the section on on-ramps for active strategic reading in chapter 5 of this workbook.

As you read the following passage, circle any words you do not know, and then look them up. Pay particular attention to the word *modicum*. What does it mean? How do you know?

> **Square Foot Gardening methods save precious resources and help in the fight against climate change. These are low-cost, low-effort, space-saving methods of gardening that can be instituted just about anywhere, with a bare modicum of resources. Because of its rapid expansion and extensive humanitarian programs, Square Foot Gardening Foundation now reaches out to . . . sources of additional funding to help sustain its global and local initiatives.**

Source: Bartholomew, Mel. *All New Square Foot Gardening: The Revolutionary Way to Grow More in Less Space*, 2nd ed., Cool Springs Press, 2013, p. 29.

_____

_____

_____

_____

_____

Exercise 14-d
Examining a reader's annotations

Name		
Date		Section

To read about this topic, see the section on on-ramps for active strategic reading in chapter 5 of this workbook.

In a pair or group, study the following excerpt from a scholarly article describing a study of distracted driving. Read both the article and the student reader's annotations in the margin; then discuss the on-ramps used by the reader.

Excerpt from "Texting at the Light and Other Forms of Device Distraction behind the Wheel"

Cell phones are a well-known source of distraction for drivers (Redelmeier and Tibshirani). According to Strayer et al., the impairments associated with using a cell phone behind the wheel are on par with those of drunk driving ("Comparison"), and the US National Safety Council has implicated device usage in 26% of all vehicular crashes. The proliferation of text messaging services, web browsers and interactive apps makes modern devices even more distracting than voice-only cell phones. One may expect that as new features are added in years to come, devices will provide an even greater temptation for drivers to divert their attention from the primary task of operating their vehicles safely (Rowden and Watson).

main idea

on par = equal

compares distracted driving with drunk driving

rapid excessive increase (a negative word)

It should be intuitively apparent that manual interaction with a device while driving a moving vehicle will be dangerous. This claim is supported by studies that found that text-messaging was associated with more driving errors (Drews et al. and Mouloua et al.) and crashes (Issar et al.). Yet even with the vehicle at rest, interacting with a device may impose risks: the driver may not be able to respond quickly enough to sudden changes in road conditions, such as an ambulance passing through. In addition, texting may produce a lingering distraction that persists even after the device is put down (Strayer et al. "Distraction"). This loss of so-called "situational awareness" is reflected in an anecdote shared by a colleague (Endsley). He reported checking a text message while sitting at the light. After looking up and noticing that the light had turned green, he rushed to accelerate—and promptly rear-ended the car in front of him, which had been slower to take off. Without situational awareness, "the drivers' eyes may be on the

easy to see, figure out

examples of distracted driving in this paragraph

specialized term

story

roadway and their hands on the steering wheel, but they may not be attending to the information critical for safe driving," as Strayer put it ("Technology").

context clue—awareness of situation and surroundings while driving

Interacting with a device with the vehicle temporarily at rest may represent a distinct form of driver distraction. Nonetheless, to our knowledge, a direct comparison of the rate of device usage by drivers at rest with the rate of device usage by drivers in motion has not been reported.

lots of examples but no study of drivers at rest vs. in motion

Significant usage differences between drivers at rest and drivers in motion, in turn, might have important implications for possible interventions aimed at decreasing this activity: if nothing else, safety processes that automatically shut down devices when the vehicle begins moving will not address texting at the light.

The research question we therefore address in this study is as follows: What is the incidence of texting with the vehicle at rest as compared with texting while the vehicle is moving? (For brevity, we will designate manual interaction with a device as "texting," though checking email, web surfing and other related activities would be included in this category.)

does device safety not work at light? reason for study

these activities define "manual interaction"

To answer the research question, we measured the rate of device usage for a set of vehicles stopped at a busy intersection, and (compared) it with the rate of device usage in a second set of vehicles that were in motion on the same road at a point just beyond that intersection.

key word, purpose of study

Source: Bernstein, James J., and Joseph Bernstein. "Texting at the Light and Other Forms of Device Distraction behind the Wheel." *BMC Public Health,* vol. 15, 2015, doi:10.1186/s12889-015-2343-8.

How is your group's analysis of the passage an example of active strategic reading?

_____

_____

_____

_____

_____

_____

Exercise 14-e
Using on-ramps to annotate and understand a reading

Name	
Date	Section

To read about this topic, see the section on on-ramps for active strategic reading in chapter 5 of this workbook.

Use active strategic reading on-ramps to mark up the following reading and build an understanding of the article's meaning and message.

"Melting Ice Could Cause More California Droughts"

Loss of ice cover in the Arctic could spur more droughts in California, according to a new study by federal researchers. The study, published today in *Nature Communications*, finds that sea-ice loss in the Arctic could trigger atmospheric effects that drive precipitation away from California. The research was led by atmospheric scientists at the Lawrence Livermore National Laboratory.

It's the same kind of effect that contributed to [the] state's historic dry period that ended last year. The five-year drought was exacerbated by an atmospheric pressure system in the North Pacific Ocean that researchers dubbed the "ridiculously resilient ridge," which pushed storms farther north and deprived the Southwest of precipitation.

"[S]ea-ice loss of the magnitude expected in the next decades could substantially impact California's precipitation, thus highlighting another mechanism by which human-caused climate change could exacerbate future California droughts," the study says.

The study stops short of attributing California's latest drought to changes in Arctic sea ice, partly because there are other phenomena that play a role, like warm sea surface temperatures and changes to the Pacific Decadal Oscillation, an atmospheric climate pattern that typically shifts every 20 to 30 years.

The recent drought is also outside the study's scope because the researchers focused on potentially larger losses in sea ice than have occurred to date. The authors predict that over the next 20 years, California could see a 10 to 15 percent decrease in rainfall on average.

"The recent California drought appears to be a good illustration of what the sea-ice drive precipitation could look like," lead researcher Ivana Cvijanovic said in a release. "While more research should be done, we should be aware that an increasing number of studies, including this one, suggest that the loss of Arctic sea ice cover is not only a problem for remote Arctic communities, but could affect millions of people worldwide."

Conversely, sea-ice loss in the Antarctic would be expected to increase California's precipitation, according to the study's modeling. The North Pacific atmospheric ridge would be replaced by a trough, encouraging tropical storms to develop over the state.

Previous studies have hypothesized that the North Pacific atmospheric ridge is caused by increased ocean surface temperatures and movement of heat in the tropical Pacific. The new study elaborates on that understanding by describing the link between Arctic sea-ice loss and tropical convection.

The study could help narrow the range of uncertainty around how climate change is expected to alter California's precipitation patterns. Better modeling of Arctic sea-ice changes could improve prediction of changes in rainfall, the researchers said.

Source: Kahn, Debra. "Melting Ice Could Cause More California Droughts." *Climate Wire,* 5 Dec. 2017, E&E News, www.eenews.net/stories /1060068087.

Exercise 14-f
Talking back to a reading

Name	
Date	Section

To read about this topic and see an example of the strategy, see section 5g in this workbook.

For the reading on pages 129–130, "Melting Ice Could Cause More California Droughts," create a double-entry notebook page to identify specific passages and talk back to the author about the text, as a way to start an academic conversation.

Ideas/passages from the text	My responses/questions

Thesis statement exercises

Exercise 15-a
Choosing effective thesis statements

An effective thesis statement is debatable, is usually an answer to a question or a solution to a problem, and uses specific language. From each of the following pairs, choose the better thesis statement for a first-year college essay. Explain your reasoning for each choice.

1.   a.   According to novelist John Steinbeck, why is it so important to have dreams and aspirations?

      b.   John Steinbeck's novel *Of Mice and Men* teaches us, perhaps better than any other novel, how our dreams and aspirations sustain us in hard times.

_____

_____

_____

_____

2.   a.   An unused three-acre parcel of land behind the local high school has been evaluated for possible uses, including co-operative farming.

      b.   It makes both economic and environmental sense to convert the unused three-acre parcel behind the local high school to a farm co-op.

_____

_____

_____

_____

3. a. In the wake of claims of racism by black and Latino artists, the music industry must act responsibly to reevaluate its guidelines for explicit content.

    b. The music industry's racist practices require explicit content advisory labels on music by black and Latino artists almost three times as often as on music by white artists.

    _____

    _____

    _____

    _____

4. a. The electoral college protects voters in rural and small states, and for this reason, the system must remain in place; moving to a popular vote system would create a sharp and undemocratic imbalance.

    b. The electoral college was designed for a number of practical reasons; one was to protect the interests of voters in rural states and small states.

    _____

    _____

    _____

    _____

5. a. Though it may seem drastic, classifying domestic violence as a hate crime, one that comes with far more serious penalties for perpetrators, is a useful step we should take to decrease domestic violence incidents.

    b. Decreasing the number of domestic violence incidents nationwide is an important goal, and new ideas about how to achieve it are critical.

    _____

    _____

    _____

    _____

6. a. In the film *Three Billboards Outside Ebbing, Missouri*, Mildred Hayes and Officer Dixon become unlikely allies—ultimately leaving viewers with hope even though the story's crime remains unsolved.

   b. In the film *Three Billboards Outside Ebbing, Missouri*, the relationship between Mildred Hayes and Officer Dixon is very interesting.

   _____

   _____

   _____

   _____

7. a. Lowering the drinking age from 21 to 18 is a bad idea.

   b. Lowering the drinking age from 21 to 18 is a workable idea only if paired with a drinker education program modeled on the classroom portion of a driver education program.

   _____

   _____

   _____

   _____

8. a. Because so many high school students cannot afford the tutoring that research has shown raises SAT and ACT scores, colleges and universities should remove these scores from their admissions evaluation criteria.

   b. It is unfortunate that so many high school students cannot afford the tutoring that research has shown raises SAT and ACT scores.

   _____

   _____

   _____

   _____

Exercise 15-b
Writing a thesis statement
for an argument essay

Name		
Date	Section	

The following brief argumentative essay includes no introductory paragraph and no thesis statement. Write a suitable thesis statement that includes the topic, a position, and some sense of the reasoning used in the argument. Once you've drafted a thesis statement, see if you can complete the checklist that follows the essay.

As an extra challenge, you might write an entire opening paragraph that includes a thesis statement.

_____

_____

_____

_____

_____

_____

_____

_____

_____

   Telehealth is an exchange of data between patients and health care providers. A typical telehealth system involves two components, the first of which is a home monitoring unit. Patients use this technology to collect information such as their weight, temperature, heart rate, blood pressure, and oxygen level. The other component is a centralized monitoring station in a doctor's office or the office of a home health provider; this station collects the data and delivers it for a health care provider to review.

   Telehealth monitoring allows elderly patients to receive health care without leaving home. The system allows them to communicate with a nurse remotely. Even though some might argue that it's healthier for elderly patients to be more mobile and to take more opportunities to leave their residence, a digital health system allows patients the flexibility to receive care even when they choose to stay home—when the weather is bad, perhaps, or when they are not feeling well enough to travel.

   Digital monitoring can also help elderly patients and their family caregivers to be more involved in managing the patient's condition. Being involved in daily checks of vital signs can give both patients and family members peace of mind.

Often families of elderly patients report feeling helpless, especially if they are not able to attend occasional doctor visits with the patient. The telehealth system engages patients and family members and often facilitates a better understanding of the patient's condition.

Most importantly, a digital health system allows changes in treatment to happen sooner, which can often keep an elderly patient out of the hospital. The quick response is both a health benefit and an economic benefit for patients. When patients don't have to wait hours or days or longer to see a clinician, their chances of maintaining good health go up, and their out-of-pocket costs go down.

Thesis statement checklist

_____ Does the thesis present a debatable point? *The thesis should not be a fact or description.*

_____ Does the thesis present an answer to a question? *The thesis should not be a question.*

_____ Is the thesis of appropriate scope for the assignment? *The thesis should not be too broad or too narrow.*

_____ Is the thesis sharply focused? *The thesis should not contain vague words like "interesting," "good," "bad," or "wrong."*

Exercise 15-c
Building strong thesis statements

Name	
Date	Section

For each of the following topics, develop a thesis statement that could work for an argument essay for a first-year writing course. You may find the checklist in Exercise 15-b helpful as you draft.

1. Concussions in college athletes

    _____

    _____

    _____

    _____

    _____

2. Student loan debt

    _____

    _____

    _____

    _____

3. Body cameras for police officers

    _____

    _____

    _____

    _____

    _____

4. Job interviews

    _____

    _____

    _____

    _____

5. Access to guns

_____

_____

_____

_____

_____

6. Film trilogies

_____

_____

_____

_____

_____

7. Learning to drive

_____

_____

_____

_____

_____

8. Using mobile payment apps such as Venmo

_____

_____

_____

_____

_____

CHAPTER 16

Topic sentence exercises

An effective topic sentence summarizes a paragraph's main point. Topic sentences help writers organize their ideas, but they also play two important roles for readers— they act as a preview for the ideas to come and as a kind of "glue" that helps readers understand the paragraph's point or its role in the whole essay.

Like a thesis statement, a topic sentence is more general than the material supporting it. Usually a writer presents a topic sentence first in the paragraph and then follows the general topic sentence with more specific material that supports it.

> **In his "Letter from Birmingham Jail," civil rights leader Martin Luther King Jr. points out examples of civil disobedience throughout history.** Early Christians in the Roman Empire, for instance, refused to renounce their faith and were persecuted. He also points to American colonists who threw tea overboard in defiance of the unjust laws of the British. Finally, he celebrates those who "aided and comforted" Jews during the Holocaust, a series of events that, at the time, were completely legal.

Good writers preview their ideas with clues for readers, key words that announce what ideas will follow. The key words in the topic sentence above are "examples of civil disobedience" and "history." After reading just the topic sentence, you can guess that the paragraph is going to cover one or more instances of civil disobedience and one or more historical time periods.

Exercise 16-a
Choosing suitable topic sentences

Name		
Date		Section

1. Read the following paragraph, which does not include a topic sentence. Then, from the choices below, identify the statement that would be the most successful topic sentence for this paragraph.

    First, increased perspiration could be a telltale sign of lying. Polygraph machines actually measure perspiration. A second giveaway relates to the touching of the face and nose. A person who is lying will experience an increased itching in the nose due to adrenaline. Finally, a quick and fleeting microexpression, such as the drawing upward of the eyebrows, could suggest that someone is not being truthful.

    a. Physical signs can suggest whether or not a person is lying.

    b. Physical signs can suggest whether or not a person is telling the truth.

    c. Law enforcement uses advanced technology to detect lying.

    d. A psychologist can detect lying roughly 90 percent of the time.

    Why did you choose the answer you did?

    _____

    _____

    _____

    _____

    _____

    _____

2. Read the following paragraph, which does not include a topic sentence. Then, from the choices below, identify the statement that would be the most successful topic sentence for this paragraph.

    One of the earliest superheroes in pop culture, Superman, first created in the 1930s, is sent as an infant to live on another planet. It's clear from early on that he doesn't blend in with his peers. Similarly, Black Widow is a Russian assassin forced to trade meaningful relationships for loyalty and duty to country. And Captain America awakens half a century in the future to an America completely unrecognizable to him. We love these characters for their "super" qualities but also for their vulnerabilities.

    a. Superhero movies appeal to viewers of all ages.

    b. Because they are detached emotionally, superheroes are better at protecting ordinary citizens.

c. Part of the emotional appeal of superhero characters stems from their depiction as outsiders and loners.

d. Part of the emotional appeal of superhero characters stems from their deep patriotism.

Why did you choose the answer you did?

_____

_____

_____

_____

_____

_____

Exercise 16-b
Writing topic sentences

Name	
Date	Section

1. The following paragraph is incomplete. Complete the paragraph by writing a suitable topic sentence.

   _____

   _____

   _____ A 30-minute mid-day nap can be a stress reliever and can work just as well for college students as music or exercise. Even more importantly, naps can improve learning and academic performance (Weir, 48). Although some people feel that napping in the afternoon is a sign of laziness, it may actually be a sign that a student is more industrious and hard-working than his or her peers. The mid-day nap refreshes the brain for an extended period of focused study.

2. The following paragraph is incomplete. Complete the paragraph by writing a suitable topic sentence.

   _____

   _____

   _____ First, many Afghan girls are part of families that have been displaced by war and poverty, and so access to schools is limited or just not a priority. Second, attitudes toward the education of girls in Afghanistan are still extremely conservative, despite the awareness raised in recent years by human rights groups and other education advocates. Finally, even when girls are enrolled in schools, they face the real possibility of physical and sexual violence as they make the trek from home to school, often with no transportation.

Exercise 16-c
Writing unified paragraphs

Paragraphs are unified when they develop a single topic and when all of the ideas support the topic sentence. For each of the following topic sentences, develop a paragraph that demonstrates unity.

1. Musicians have always written songs about love. _____

_____

_____

_____

_____

_____

_____

_____

_____

_____

2. Sleep deprivation can have disastrous effects on college students' lives. _____

_____

_____

_____

_____

_____

_____

_____

_____

_____

3. There are important differences between having a job and having a career. _____

_____

_____

_____

_____

_____

_____

_____

_____

CHAPTER 17

PART 3

MLA research exercises

Exercise 17-a
Avoiding plagiarism in MLA papers

Name	
Date	Section

For help with this exercise, see the section on avoiding plagiarism in MLA papers in your handbook.

Read the following passage and the information about its source. Then decide whether each student sample is plagiarized or uses the source correctly. If the student's sample is plagiarized, write "plagiarized"; if the sample is acceptable, write "OK."

ORIGINAL SOURCE

> Smartphone games are built on a very different model [from traditional video games]. The iPhone's screen is roughly the size of a playing card; it responds not to the fast-twitch button combos of a controller but to more intuitive and intimate motions: poking, pinching, tapping, tickling. This has encouraged a very different kind of game: Tetris-like little puzzles, broken into discrete bits, designed to be played anywhere, in any context, without a manual, by any level of player. (Charles Pratt, a researcher in New York University's Game Center, refers to such games as "knitting games.") You could argue that these are pure games: perfectly designed minisystems engineered to take us directly to the core of gaming pleasure without the distraction of narrative.
>
> *Source:* Anderson, Sam. "Just One More Game. . . ." *The New York Times Magazine*, 4 Apr. 2012, nyti.ms/1AZ2pys.

1. Smartphone screens have encouraged a new type of intimate game, broken into discrete bits, that can be played by anyone, anywhere. _____

2. The smartphone touchscreen has changed the nature of video games: Instead of "fast-twitch button combos," touchscreens use "intuitive and intimate motions" such as "poking [and] pinching" (Anderson). _____

3. As Sam Anderson explains, games on smartphones are "designed to be played anywhere, in any context, without a manual, by any level of player."

    _____

4. Sam Anderson points out that, unlike older, narrative-based games that required a controller, games played on smartphone touchscreens can be learned quickly by anyone, regardless of skill level. _____

5. Smartphone games can be called "perfectly designed minisystems" because they bring us right into the game "without the distraction of narrative." _____

Exercise 17-b
Avoiding plagiarism in MLA papers

Name

Date

Section

For help with this exercise, see the section on avoiding plagiarism in MLA papers in your handbook.

Read the following passage and the information about its source. Then decide whether each student sample is plagiarized or uses the source correctly. If the student's sample is plagiarized, write "plagiarized"; if the sample is acceptable, write "OK."

ORIGINAL SOURCE

We probably spend more time thinking and talking about other people than anything else. If another person makes us exuberantly happy, furiously angry, or deeply sad, we often can't stop thinking about him or her. We will often drop his or her name in our conversations with others, tossing in numerous pronouns as we refer to the person. Consequently, if the speaker is thinking and talking about a friend, expect high rates of third-person singular pronouns. If worried about communists, right-wing radio hosts, or bureaucrats, words such as *they* and *them* will be more frequent than average.

The word *I* is no different. If people are self-conscious, their attention flips to themselves briefly but at higher rates than people who are not self-conscious. For example, people use the word *I* more when completing a questionnaire in front of a mirror than if no mirror is present. If their attention is drawn to themselves because they are sick, feeling pain, or deeply depressed, they also use *I* more. In contrast, people who are immersed in a task tend to use I-words at very low levels.

Source: Pennebaker, James W. *The Secret Life of Pronouns: What Our Words Say about Us.* Bloomsbury Press, 2011. [The source passage is from pages 291–92. Page 291 ends after *Consequently*, at the start of the fourth sentence.]

1. Adults spend more time thinking and talking about other people than they spend on anything else. _____

2. High levels of emotion about someone may cause us to refer to that person more often and to use "numerous pronouns as we refer to the person" (Pennebaker 291).

   _____

3. Pennebaker notes that people talking about friends will use "high rates of third-person singular pronouns," whereas plural pronouns "such as *they* and *them* will be more frequent than average" when people are talking about certain groups that might make them uncomfortable (292). _____

4. Pennebaker explains that self-conscious people use *I* more often because "their attention flips to themselves at higher rates than people who are not self-conscious" (292). _____

5. Pennebaker suggests that we can understand the way speakers regard those whom they are talking about by analyzing the pronouns the speakers use most frequently (291–92). _____

Exercise 17-c
Recognizing common knowledge in MLA papers

Name	
Date	Section

For help with this exercise, see the section on recognizing common knowledge in MLA papers in your handbook.

Read each student passage and determine whether the student needs to cite the source of the information in an MLA paper. If the material does not need citation because it is common knowledge, write "common knowledge." If the material is not common knowledge and the student should cite the source, write "needs citation."

EXAMPLE

The playwright August Wilson won two Pulitzer Prizes in drama. *Common knowledge*

[Winners of well-known prizes such as the Pulitzer Prize are common

knowledge because the information is readily available in any number

of sources.]

1. Many of William Faulkner's novels are set in Yoknapatawpha County, a fictional part of Mississippi. _____

2. William Faulkner may have gotten the word *Yoknapatawpha* from a 1915 dictionary of the Choctaw language. _____

3. The writer and folklorist Zora Neale Hurston died in poverty in 1960. _____

4. William Shakespeare was the only playwright of his generation known to have a long-standing relationship with a single theater company. _____

5. Walt Disney fired and blacklisted all of his animators who went on strike in 1941. _____

6. William Wordsworth and Percy Bysshe Shelley were poets of the Romantic era. _____

7. As of 2012, the film *Titanic* had earned more than two billion dollars in box office revenue worldwide. _____

8. Heroic couplets are rhyming pairs of lines written in iambic pentameter. _____

9. Iris Murdoch wrote many sophisticated and complex novels before she succumbed to Alzheimer's disease. _____

10. George Lucas made a larger fortune by selling *Star Wars* toys than he made by selling tickets to *Star Wars*. _____

Exercise 17-d
Integrating sources in MLA papers

For help with this exercise, see the section on integrating sources in MLA papers in your handbook.

Read the following passage and the information about its source. Then decide whether each student sample uses the source correctly. If the student has made an error in using the source, revise the sample to avoid the error. If the student has quoted correctly, write "OK."

ORIGINAL SOURCE

   More than 1% of California's electricity comes from the wind. During breezy early mornings in summer, the contribution goes even higher. "At those times, the wind accounts for up to 8% of our electrical load," said Mary A. Ilyin, a wind researcher for Pacific Gas & Electric, the country's largest utility and a major booster of wind power.

   Half of California's turbines . . . are located in Altamont Pass and feed directly into PG&E's grid. Most of the rest are found in two other major wind centers: Tehachapi Pass on the edge of the Mojave Desert between Bakersfield and Barstow, with a capacity of 458 megawatts, and San Gorgonio Pass north of Palm Springs (231 megawatts). Both are hooked up to the power lines of Southern California Edison.

Source: Golden, Frederic. "Electric Wind." *Los Angeles Times*, 24 Dec. 1990, p. B1.

1. Wind power accounts for more than 1% of California's electricity, reports Frederic Golden, and during breezy early mornings in summer, the contribution goes even higher (B1).

     _____

     _____

     _____

2. According to Frederic Golden, wind power accounts for more than 1% of California's electricity, and on breezy days "the contribution goes even higher" (B1).

     _____

     _____

     _____

3.   Mary A. Ilyin reports that "wind energy accounts for as much as 8% of California's electricity" (qtd. in Golden B1).

_____

_____

_____

4.   On breezy summer mornings, says wind researcher Mary A. Ilyin, "the wind accounts for up to 8% of our [California's] electrical load" (qtd. in Golden B1).

_____

_____

_____

5.   California has pioneered the use of wind power. "Half of California's turbines . . . are located in Altamont Pass" (Golden B1).

_____

_____

_____

Exercise 17-e
Integrating sources in MLA papers

Name	
Date	Section

For help with this exercise, see the section on integrating sources in MLA papers in your handbook.

Read the following passage and the information about its source. Then decide whether each student sample uses the source correctly. If the student has made an error in using the source, revise the sample to avoid the error. If the student has quoted correctly, write "OK."

ORIGINAL SOURCE

Most of us think that S.U.V.s are much safer than sports cars. If you asked the young parents of America whether they would rather strap their infant child in the back seat of the TrailBlazer [a Chevrolet S.U.V.] or the passenger seat of the Boxster [a Porsche sports car], they would choose the TrailBlazer. We feel that way because in the TrailBlazer our chances of surviving a collision with a hypothetical tractor-trailer in the other lane are greater than they are in the Porsche. What we forget, though, is that in the TrailBlazer you're also much more likely to hit the tractor-trailer because you can't get out of the way in time. In the parlance of the automobile world, the TrailBlazer is better at "passive safety." The Boxster is better when it comes to "active safety," which is every bit as important.

Source: Gladwell, Malcolm. "Big and Bad." *The New Yorker*, 12 Jan. 2004, pp. 28–33. [The source passage is from page 31.]

1. Malcolm Gladwell points out that drivers feel safer in an S.U.V. than in a sports car because they think that the S.U.V. driver's "chances of surviving a collision with a hypothetical tractor-trailer in the other lane are greater" (31).

    _____

    _____

    _____

2. Gladwell argues that "active safety is every bit as important" as a vehicle's ability to withstand a collision (31).

    _____

    _____

    _____

3. A majority of drivers can, indeed, be wrong. "Most of us think that S.U.V.s are much safer than sports cars" (Gladwell 31).

    _____

    _____

    _____

4. According to Gladwell, American S.U.V.s are more likely to be involved in collisions than other vehicles "because [they] can't get out of the way in time" (31).

    _____

    _____

    _____

5. Gladwell explains that most people expect an S.U.V. "to survive a collision with a hypothetical tractor-trailer in the other lane" (31).

    _____

    _____

    _____

Exercise 17-f
MLA documentation: In-text citations

Name

Date

Section

For help with this exercise, see the MLA in-text citations section in your handbook.

Circle the letter of the MLA in-text citation that is handled correctly.

EXAMPLE

The student is quoting from pages 26–27 of the following source:

Follman, Mark. "Trigger Warnings." *Mother Jones*, Nov./Dec. 2015, pp. 22–29.

(a.) Mass shootings in America took a turn with Columbine; Follman argues that the teen shooters "authored a compelling new script at the dawn of the Internet age" (26–27).

b. Mass shootings in America took a turn with Columbine; Follman argues that the teen shooters "authored a compelling new script at the dawn of the Internet age" (pp. 26–27).

1. The student is quoting Christina Hoff Sommers from page 17 of the following book:

    Winegarner, Beth. *The Columbine Effect: How Five Teen Pastimes Got Caught in the Crossfire.* Lulu Press, 2013.

    a. In the wake of Columbine, according to Christina Hoff Sommers, "It has become fashionable to attribute pathology to millions of healthy male children" (qtd. in Winegarner 17).

    b. In the wake of Columbine, according to Christina Hoff Sommers, "It has become fashionable to attribute pathology to millions of healthy male children" (17).

2. The student is citing a blog post that appeared on the *Psychology Today* website:

    Ramsland, Katherine. "Mass Murder Motives." *Psychology Today*, 20 July 2012, www.psychologytoday.com/blog/shadow-boxing/201207/mass-murder-motives.

    a. Katherine Ramsland describes motives for mass murder that "rang[e] from revenge to despair to free-floating rage at the world" ("Mass").

    b. Katherine Ramsland describes motives for mass murder that "rang[e] from revenge to despair to free-floating rage at the world."

3. The student is quoting from page 472 of a scholarly article by Dianne T. Gereluk, Kent Donlevy, and Merlin B. Thompson.

   a. Gereluk, Donlevy, and Thompson have called the teacher's threat assessment role "onerous" and have expressed concern about the "tremendous burden of watching for potential threats" in and out of the classroom (472).

   b. Gereluk et al. have called the teacher's threat assessment role "onerous" and have expressed concern about the "tremendous burden of watching for potential threats" in and out of the classroom (472).

4. The student is using statistics from the following article:

   Follman, Mark. "Trigger Warnings." *Mother Jones*, Nov./Dec. 2015, pp. 22–29.

   a. In the seventy-two known Columbine copycat cases, 53% of the planned attacks involved guns, and 18% involved bombs or explosives (Follman 27).

   b. In the seventy-two known Columbine copycat cases, 53% of the planned attacks involved guns, and 18% involved bombs or explosives.

5. The student is summarizing information gathered from a map found in this source:

   Mosendz, Polly. "Map: Every School Shooting in America since 2013." *Newsweek*, 16 Oct. 2015, www.newsweek.com/list-school-shootings-america-2013-380535.

   a. An analysis of the map reveals that there is no regional concentration in the occurrence of school shootings. They happen everywhere in America ("Map").

   b. An analysis of the map reveals that there is no regional concentration in the occurrence of school shootings. They happen everywhere in America (Mosendz).

6. The student is quoting the author's exact words from this online video:

   Gladwell, Malcolm. "Malcolm Gladwell Discusses School Shootings." *YouTube*, 5 Oct. 2015, www.youtube.com/watch?v=27aWHudLmgs.

   a. Gladwell's assessment of the recent history of school shootings is eye-opening: "It's an overwhelmingly American phenomenon," he says.

   b. Gladwell's assessment of the recent history of school shootings is eye-opening: It's an overwhelmingly American phenomenon, he says.

7. The student is summarizing the following unsigned source:

   "Another Day, Another Tragic School Shooting." *The Washington Post*, 9 Oct. 2015, www.washingtonpost.com/opinions/another-day-another-tragic-school -shooting/2015/10/09/62f5077c-6eb5-11e5-b31c-d80d62b53e28_story.html .Editorial.

a. Mental health treatment and peer counseling are good first steps to reducing school violence; restricting access to guns, however, is the most important step (Editorial).

b. Mental health treatment and peer counseling are good first steps to reducing school violence; restricting access to guns, however, is the most important step ("Another").

8. The student is quoting from page 45 of the following source:

Klein, Jessie. *The Bully Society: School Shootings and the Crisis of Bullying in America's Schools.* New York UP, 2013.

The list of works cited in the student's paper includes two works by Klein.

a. Klein, a sociology professor, raises the idea that "boys are pressured to behave in a host of essentially superhuman or nonhuman ways" (*Bully* 45).

b. Klein, a sociology professor, raises the idea that "boys are pressured to behave in a host of essentially superhuman or nonhuman ways" (45).

9. The student is paraphrasing from this short work from a website:

"Effects of Bullying." *StopBullying.gov*, US Department of Health and Human Services, www.stopbullying.gov/at-risk/effects/. Accessed 5 Apr. 2016.

a. Violence against others can be a response to being chronically bullied. There is evidence that many school shooters and mass shooters have experienced bullying (US Department of Health and Human Services).

b. Violence against others can be a response to being chronically bullied. There is evidence that many school shooters and mass shooters have experienced bullying ("Effects").

10. The student is quoting from a blog post:

Brucculieri, Julia, and Cole Delbyck. "These Classic TV Episodes about School Shootings Are More Relevant Than Ever." *Huffington Post*, 24 Jan. 2016, www.huffingtonpost.com/entry/school-shootings-on-tv_us_56a14986e4b076aadcc5c94b?utm_hp_ref=school-shooting.

a. *Huffington Post* entertainment bloggers posted that a 2013 episode of *Glee* led some viewers to "[draw] connections between autism and Newtown, Connecticut, shooter Adam Lanza" and the show's Becky character (Brucculieri and Delbyck).

b. *Huffington Post* entertainment bloggers posted that a 2013 episode of *Glee* led some viewers to "[draw] connections between autism and Newtown, Connecticut, shooter Adam Lanza" and the show's Becky character (Brucculieri).

For help with this exercise, see the MLA works cited section in your handbook.

Circle the letter of the works cited entry that is handled correctly.

EXAMPLE

The student has paraphrased information from the book *Breach of Faith: Hurricane Katrina and the Near Death of a Great American City*, by Jed Horne. The book was published in New York in 2008 by Random House.

a.   Horne, Jed. *Breach of Faith: Hurricane Katrina and the Near Death of a Great American City.* New York, Random House, 2008.

(b.) Horne, Jed. *Breach of Faith: Hurricane Katrina and the Near Death of a Great American City.* Random House, 2008.

1. The student has quoted from an article about Hurricane Sandy in the January 2013 issue of *Runner's World*. The article, "The Storm [and Everything After]," which appeared on pages 68–69, has no author listed.

    a.   Anonymous. "The Storm [and Everything After]." *Runner's World*, Jan. 2013, pp. 68–69.

    b.   "The Storm [and Everything After]." *Runner's World*, Jan. 2013, pp. 68–69.

2. The student has quoted from an article titled "The Katrina Conspiracies: The Problem of Trust in Rebuilding an American City," which was published in volume 35, issue 2, of *Journal of Urban History* in January 2009. The article appeared on pages 207–19 and was accessed using the *Academic OneFile* database at the URL go.galegroup.com.ezproxy.bpl.org/. The authors of the article are Arnold R. Hirsch and Lee A. Levert.

    a.   Hirsch, Arnold R., and Lee A. Levert. "The Katrina Conspiracies: The Problem of Trust in Rebuilding an American City." *Journal of Urban History*, volume 35, number 2, 2009, pp. 207–19.

    b.   Hirsch, Arnold R., and Lee A. Levert. "The Katrina Conspiracies: The Problem of Trust in Rebuilding an American City." *Journal of Urban History*, vol. 35, no. 2, 2009, pp. 207–19. *Academic OneFile*, go.galegroup.com.ezproxy.bpl.org/.

3. The student has paraphrased information from an article titled "Hurricane Katrina as a Bureaucratic Nightmare," written by Vicki Bier. The article appeared on pages 243–54 of the anthology *On Risk and Disaster: Lessons from Hurricane Katrina*. The anthology was edited by Ronald J. Daniels, Donald F. Kettl, and

Howard Kunreuther and was published in 2006 by the University of Pennsylvania Press.

a. Bier, Vicki. "Hurricane Katrina as a Bureaucratic Nightmare." *On Risk and Disaster: Lessons from Hurricane Katrina*, edited by Ronald J. Daniels et al., U of Pennsylvania P, 2006, pp. 243–54.

b. Daniels, Ronald J., et al., editors. *On Risk and Disaster: Lessons from Hurricane Katrina*. Vicki Bier, "Hurricane Katrina as a Bureaucratic Nightmare," U of Pennsylvania P, 2006, pp. 243–54.

4. The student has quoted information from a newspaper article that appeared in print on July 13, 2012, in *The Gardner News*. The article, written by Sam Bonacci and titled "Building Haiti Clinic Adds Up to Journey for Gardner Community," begins on page 1 and continues on page 4.

a. Bonacci, Sam. "Building Haiti Clinic Adds Up to Journey for Gardner Community." *The Gardner News*, 13 July 2012, pp. 1, 4.

b. Bonacci, Sam. "Building Haiti Clinic Adds Up to Journey for Gardner Community." *The Gardner News*, 13 July 2012, pp. 1+.

5. The student has paraphrased information from the article "How Weather Could Link Japan Radiation to US," which appeared on the *Scientific American* website (www.scientificamerican.com/article/weather-japan-radiation-united-states/) on March 16, 2011. The article was written by Jim Andrews and AccuWeather.

a. Andrews, Jim, and AccuWeather. "How Weather Could Link Japan Radiation to US." *Scientific American*, 16 Mar. 2011, www.scientificamerican.com/article/weather-japan-radiation-united-states/.

b. Andrews, Jim, and AccuWeather. "How Weather Could Link Japan Radiation to US." *Scientific American*, www.scientificamerican.com/article/weather-japan-radiation-united-states/.

6. The student has summarized information from a televised interview with Fareed Zakaria, conducted by Ali Velshi. Video from the interview, titled "Was Hurricane Sandy a Wake-Up Call?," was posted on the *Your Money* blog on the CNN website at the URL yourmoney.blogs.cnn.com/2012/11/23/was-hurricane-sandy-a-wake-up-call/?hpt=ym_bn2. The interview took place on November 21, 2012.

a. Zakaria, Fareed. "Was Hurricane Sandy a Wake-Up Call?" Interview by Ali Velshi, *Your Money*, CNN, 21 Nov. 2012, yourmoney.blogs.cnn.com/2012/11/23/was-hurricane-sandy-a-wake-up-call/?hpt=ym_bn2.

b. Velshi, Ali. "Was Hurricane Sandy a Wake-Up Call?" Interviewed Fareed Zakaria, *Your Money*, CNN, 21 Nov. 2012, yourmoney.blogs.cnn.com/2012/11/23/was-hurricane-sandy-a-wake-up-call/?hpt=ym_bn2.

7. The student has paraphrased information from a film on DVD titled *Japan's Killer Quake*, which was released by PBS in 2011. The film was narrated by Corey Johnson and directed by Rae Gilder and Tom Pearson.

    a. *Japan's Killer Quake*. Directed by Rae Gilder and Tom Pearson. Narr. Corey Johnson. PBS, 2011.

    b. *Japan's Killer Quake*. Directed by Rae Gilder and Tom Pearson, narrated by Corey Johnson, PBS, 2011.

8. The student has quoted from a document *Navigating the Unknown: A Practical Lifeline for Decision-Makers in the Dark*, written by Patrick Lagadec and translated by Peter Leonard. The document was published by Crisis Response Journal in Thatcham, United Kingdom, in 2013.

    a. Lagadec, Patrick. *Navigating the Unknown: A Practical Lifeline for Decision-Makers in the Dark*. Translated by Peter Leonard, Crisis Response Journal, 2013.

    b. Lagadec, Patrick, and translated by Peter Leonard. *Navigating the Unknown: A Practical Lifeline for Decision-Makers in the Dark*, Crisis Response Journal, 2013.

9. The student has paraphrased a blog entry titled "Katrina," written by Chris Matthew Sciabarra on his blog, *Notablog*. The entry was posted at the URL www.nyu.edu/projects/sciabarra/notablog/archives/000727.html on September 6, 2005, and the student accessed it on February 2, 2009.

    a. Sciabarra, Chris Matthew. "Katrina." *Notablog*, 6 Sept. 2005, www.nyu.edu/projects/sciabarra/notablog/archives/000727.html.

    b. Sciabarra, Chris Matthew. "Katrina." *Notablog*, 6 Sept. 2005, www.nyu.edu/projects/sciabarra/notablog/archives/000727.html. Accessed 2 Feb. 2009.

10. The student has summarized information from an article on the web titled "Post-Katrina Education Problems Linger." The article appeared on the website *eSchool News* on August 30, 2007, at the URL http://www.eschoolnews.com/2007/08/30/post-katrina-education-problems-linger/. No author is given.

    a. "Post-Katrina Education Problems Linger." *eSchool News*, 30 Aug. 2007.

    b. "Post-Katrina Education Problems Linger." *eSchool News*, 30 Aug. 2007, www.eschoolnews.com/2007/08/30/post-katrina-education-problems-linger/.

Exercise 17-h
MLA documentation

Name

Date | Section

For help with this exercise, see the sections on MLA documentation in your handbook.

Write "true" if the statement is true or "false" if it is false.

1. A parenthetical citation in the text of a paper must always include a URL if the source is from the web. _____

2. The works cited list is organized alphabetically by authors' last names (or by title for a work with no author). _____

3. When in-text citations are used throughout a paper, there is no need for a works cited list at the end of the paper. _____

4. An in-text citation names the author (if there is an author) either in a signal phrase introducing the cited material or in parentheses after the cited material. _____

5. When a work's author is unknown, the work is listed under "Anonymous" in the list of works cited. _____

6. All authors are listed last name first, followed by first name, in the works cited list. _____

7. When a work has no page number, it is possible that nothing will appear in parentheses to mark the end of a citation. _____

8. In the parentheses marking the end of an in-text citation, the abbreviation "p." or "pp." is used before the page number or numbers. _____

9. When a paper cites two or more works by the same author, the in-text citation includes at least the author's name and the title (or a short version of the title). _____

10. For a works cited entry for a web source, a permalink (static, permanent link) or DOI (digital object identifier) is preferable to a URL. _____

CHAPTER 18

PART 3

Plagiarism exercises

Exercise 18-a
Is this plagiarism?

Name	
Date	Section

In preparation for this activity, read the sections on avoiding plagiarism in your handbook. Also read the material on plagiarism (it could be called "integrity" or "academic honesty") on your school's website or the English department's website.

For each of the following scenarios, argue whether or not the student plagiarized.

1. Student A has just begun to work on a research essay. The length requirement for this essay is four to six pages. It is now the night before the essay is due, and the student has written only two pages. To fill in the rest, he goes to several different websites and copies and pastes paragraphs from them into the body of his essay. He does not change the words, and he does not put the paragraphs in quotation marks. He does, however, list a couple of the websites on his works cited page.

    Is Student A committing plagiarism? Why or why not? _____

    _____

    _____

    _____

    _____

    _____

2. Student B is having trouble with her research essay. She has one page written, and she has found great sources, but she is having difficulty with the organizational structure of the essay. She goes to the Writing Center on campus, where a tutor helps her organize her ideas and cite her sources correctly.

    Is Student B committing plagiarism? Why or why not? _____

    _____

    _____

_____

_____

_____

3. Student C purchases an essay online. She pays the full price, and the site assures her that she now owns the essay. She puts her name on the top, prints the essay, and turns it in.

    Is Student C committing plagiarism? Why or why not? _____

    _____

    _____

    _____

    _____

    _____

4. While writing a research essay, Student D uses language directly from Wikipedia. He does not use quotation marks, but he does indicate that the language came from this website by stating in the essay, "According to Wikipedia, ..."

    Is Student D committing plagiarism? Why or why not? _____

    _____

    _____

    _____

    _____

5. Student E is writing a research essay. He goes to a website and finds a lot of great information to use in his essay. He paraphrases (puts the material in his own words), but he does not cite the source of the information or include a works cited list.

    Is Student E committing plagiarism? Why or why not? _____

    _____

    _____

    _____

    _____

    _____

Name	
Date	Section

Imagine that you are mentoring a small group of high school students. The students do not have a lot of experience with academic writing. Reflecting on your own experience, and perhaps referring to the advice in your handbook, write five tips for your students on how to become a responsible writer and avoid plagiarism.

1. _____

   _____

2. _____

   _____

3. _____

   _____

4. _____

   _____

5. _____

   _____

CHAPTER 19

PART 3

Paraphrase and summary exercises

Exercise 19-a
Building understanding (writing a summary)

Name	
Date	Section

Read the following passage three or four times; also read the title of the book that the passage is taken from. Then complete steps 1–6.

> Now just because I identify with my people doesn't mean that I don't understand and grapple with what it means to be white in America. In fact, I was trained in your schools and I now teach your children. But I remain what I was when I started my vocation, my pilgrimage of self-discovery: a black preacher. It is for that reason that I don't want to—really, I can't afford to—give up on the possibility that white America can definitively, finally, hear from one black American preacher a plea, a cry, a sermon, from my heart to yours.

Source: Dyson, Michael Eric. *Tears We Cannot Stop: A Sermon to White America.* St. Martin's Press, 2017, pp. 5–6.

1. What can you tell about this reading or its author, Michael Eric Dyson, just from the title of the book? _____

    _____

    _____

2. Make notes on the passage. Write down, circle, highlight, or define anything you think might help you understand what this passage is about.

> Now just because I identify with my people doesn't mean that I don't understand and grapple with what it means to be white in America. In fact, I was trained in your schools and I now teach your children. But I remain what I was when I started my vocation, my pilgrimage of self-discovery: a black preacher. It is for that reason that I don't want to—really, I can't afford to—give up on the possibility that white America can definitively, finally, hear from one black American preacher a plea, a cry, a sermon, from my heart to yours.

3. Read the passage and your notes one more time. Then WITHOUT LOOKING at the passage, write down the author's basic message or main idea, as you understand it.

    _____

    _____

    _____

    _____

    _____

4. Write a one-sentence summary that communicates your understanding of the author's main idea. _____

    _____

    _____

    _____

    _____

5. If you have used any exact language from Dyson's passage, go back and put those words in quotation marks.

6. You still must cite a source even if you summarize it in your own words. Add a citation at the end of your summary sentence—either the author's last name and the page numbers in parentheses or, if you mentioned the author's last name in your sentence, just the page numbers in parentheses.

Exercise 19-b
Using your own words and structure (writing a paraphrase)

Name

Date | Section

Read the following passage three or four times; also read the title of the book that the passage is taken from. Then complete steps 1–6.

> **Durable, robust learning requires that we do two things. First, as we recode and consolidate new material from short-term memory into long-term memory, we must anchor it there securely. Second, we must associate the material with a diverse set of cues that will make us adept at recalling the knowledge later. Having effective retrieval cues is an aspect of learning that often goes overlooked. The task is more than committing knowledge to memory. Being able to retrieve it when we need it is just as important.**

Source: Brown, Peter C., Henry L. Roediger III, and Mark A. McDaniel. *Make It Stick: The Science of Successful Learning.* Harvard UP, 2014, p. 75.

1. What can you tell about this reading just from the title of the book? _____

    _____

    _____

    _____

2. Make notes on the passage. Write down, circle, highlight, or define anything you think might help you understand what this passage is about.

> **Durable, robust learning requires that we do two things. First, as we recode and consolidate new material from short-term memory into long-term memory, we must anchor it there securely. Second, we must associate the material with a diverse set of cues that will make us adept at recalling the knowledge later. Having effective retrieval cues is an aspect of learning that often goes overlooked. The task is more than committing knowledge to memory. Being able to retrieve it when we need it is just as important.**

3. Read the passage and your notes one more time. Then WITHOUT LOOKING at the passage, write down the authors' basic message or main idea, as you understand it.

    _____

    _____

    _____

    _____

    _____

4. Paraphrasing a source requires you to capture the ideas from the source in roughly the same amount of words and sentences. Paraphrasing responsibly means using your own words *and* using your own sentence structure. Your paraphrase shouldn't be organized in the same way as the original, and it shouldn't just substitute occasional words for the source's words. The original passage above is six sentences. Write a paraphrase of roughly five to seven sentences using your own language and organization.

    _____

    _____

    _____

    _____

    _____

    _____

    _____

    _____

    _____

    _____

5. If you have used any exact language from the authors, go back and put those words in quotation marks.

6. You still must cite a source even if you paraphrase it in your own words. Add a citation at the end of your summary sentence—either the first author's last name and the page number in parentheses or, if you mentioned the authors in your sentence, just the page number in parentheses. (Hint: For three or more authors, use "et al." for "and others." Here's an example: Nuñez et al. 37.)

Exercise 19-c
Writing paraphrases and summaries

Name

Date

Section

Read the following passage. From the options that follow the passage, choose the summary that is written more responsibly, and explain your reasoning.

> Food companies use every means at their disposal . . . to create and protect an environment that is conducive to selling their products in a competitive marketplace. To begin with, they lobby. They lobby Congress for favorable laws, government agencies for favorable regulations, and the White House for favorable trade agreements. But lobbying is only the most obvious of their methods. Far less visible are the arrangements made with food and nutrition experts to obtain approving judgments about the nutritional quality or health benefits of food products.

Source: Nestle, Marion. *Food Politics: How the Food Industry Influences Nutrition and Health.* U of California P, 2013, p. 93.

1. a. Beyond the expected strategy, lobbying US legislators, food manufacturers also strategize to get experts in the field to say that their products are healthy and nutritious (Nestle 93).

    b. Beyond lobbying Congress for favorable laws, food manufacturers also strategize to obtain approving judgments about the nutritional quality of food from experts in the field (Nestle 93).

    Which is the more responsible summary? _____

    Explain your reasoning. _____

    _____

    _____

    _____

    _____

First, review the passage at the top of the page. Then, from the options below, choose the paraphrase that is written more responsibly, and explain your reasoning.

2. a. Policy expert Marion Nestle points out that high competition requires food manufacturers to use many different strategies. One strategy is that they lobby for trade agreements, rules, and laws that benefit their sales and marketing efforts. Another strategy, perhaps not so apparent, involves trying to get health experts to vouch for their products as healthy and beneficial (93).

b. Policy expert Marion Nestle points out that food manufacturers use many different strategies to create the best environment for their success. One strategy is that they lobby. They lobby for trade agreements, rules, and laws that benefit their sales and marketing efforts. But lobbying is only the most apparent strategy. Another strategy, perhaps not so apparent, involves trying to get health experts to pass approving judgments of the products as healthy and beneficial (93).

Which is the more responsible paraphrase? _____

Explain your reasoning. _____

_____

_____

_____

_____

Bonus: Explain why the citations in item 2 above have just a page number in parentheses while the citations in item 1 have a name and a page number. Is one style right and the other wrong? _____

_____

_____

_____

_____

## CHAPTER 20

Active verbs

Exercise 20-a
Active verbs

Name	
Date	Section

To read about this topic, see the section on active verbs in your handbook.

Half of the following sentences contain passive verbs or verbs that are a form of *be*. Find them and change them to active verbs. You may need to invent a subject for some verbs, and you may need to make major revisions in some sentences. If a sentence already contains only active verbs, mark it as "active." Example:

> P
> ~~Frederick Douglass was annoyed by~~ people who spoke openly of helping the underground
>   *annoyed Frederick Douglass.*
> railroad/
>   ^

1. Frederick Douglass said that by talking openly about it, these people had turned the "underground railroad" into an "upperground railroad."

2. Although these people were deserving of praise, their open talk endangered escaping slaves.

3. Such talk alerted slave owners to possible escape routes.

4. Escaping slaves would often be caught by professional slave hunters at the houses of those who talked openly.

5. All slaves were threatened by any information that increased slave owners' knowledge.

6. Whenever slave owners suspected some of the escape routes, the courage of the slaves was lost.

7. Frederick Douglass understood the slaves' fears very well: His first attempt to escape had failed.

8. Professional slave breakers beat and tortured captured slaves until the slaves submitted or died.

9. His own treatment at the hands of slave breakers left Douglass with severe, disfiguring scars all over his back.

10. Years later, northerners were convinced by those scars that Douglass spoke the truth about slavery.

Exercise 20-b
Active verbs

Name

Date   Section

To read about this topic, see the section on active verbs in your handbook.

Revise any weak or unemphatic sentences by replacing passive verbs, or *be* verbs, with active verbs. The first revision has been done for you.

changed some of his

~~Some of~~ Frederick Douglass's̬ ideas about the North ~~were changed~~ after his successful escape from slavery. Before that time, Douglass's assumption was that northerners lacked both money and culture. In the South, only poor people owned no slaves. Also, no lovely homes, no pianos, no art, and often no books were owned by poor people. When he first saw New Bedford, Massachusetts, Douglass was doubtful of his own eyesight. He saw no dilapidated houses or naked children or barefoot women in New Bedford. Instead, the beautiful homes with equally beautiful furniture and gardens were an indication of considerable wealth. Quality merchandise was handled by laborers on the wharves and purchased by them in the stores. When he saw all of this, Douglass happily changed his ideas about the North.

## CHAPTER 21

Parallelism

Exercise 21-a
Parallelism

Name

Date | Section

To read about this topic, see the section on parallelism in your handbook.

Circle the letter of the word or word group that best completes each sentence, giving it a parallel structure. Example:

> **Leonardo da Vinci was handsome, generous, clever, and** _____.
>
> (a.) **ambidextrous**
>
> b. **able to use either hand for most activities**
>
> c. **he could use either hand for most activities**

1. Leonardo's life had three distinct periods: his childhood in Vinci, his apprenticeship in Florence, and _____.
   a. when he was an adult
   b. his being an adult and earning his own way
   c. his adulthood in various Italian cities

2. In childhood, Leonardo had not only a loving family and relatives but also

   _____.

   a. safe and unspoiled acres to explore
   b. he had the whole gentle slope of a mountain to explore
   c. including fields and vineyards to explore

3.   However, two natural events haunted his memory for years: A hurricane
     destroyed much of the valley below his village, and _____.
     a. a flood washed away much of the city of Florence
     b. a flood that washed away much of the city of Florence
     c. the boiling, muddy, surging waters of a flood

4.   Wind and water became major topics for Leonardo's study. He decided that wind
     and water were both useful and _____.
     a. did harmful things
     b. they caused harm
     c. harmful

5.   Viewers can find in many of Leonardo's works small round pebbles washed by a
     stream, riverbanks covered with moss and flowers, and _____.
     a. little freshwater crabs partly hidden beneath rocks
     b. viewers can find small freshwater crabs under rocks
     c. little freshwater crabs sometimes hide beneath rocks

Exercise 21-b
Parallelism

To read about this topic, see the section on parallelism in your handbook.

Edit the following paragraphs to correct faulty parallelism. The first revision has been done for you.

Leonardo da Vinci's vision of life as one borderless unity affected both his personal life and ~~it affected~~ his artistic work.

Leonardo did not simply look at the world; he studied it carefully. Watching the wind ripple the water in a pond, he was observant, intent, and in a serious mood. Leonardo saw no boundaries in nature; to him, people and animals were parts of one creation. He ate no meat because he did not want to bring death to a fellow creature; he bought caged songbirds so that he could set them free. Having no family of his own, he adopted a boy from another family to be both his son and he would be his heir. Even right- and left-handedness were the same to him. He filled his notebooks with mirror writing, but he wrote letters, reports, and proposals in the usual way. When his right hand became crippled, he used his left.

Leonardo's view of all of life as one creation led him to artistic innovations. Before Leonardo, artists had always used outlines to separate a painting's subject from its background. Because Leonardo saw everything in nature as interrelated, he decided that using shadow and gradation of light and color was better than to use an outline. He wanted one thing to flow into another the way smoke flows into air. Looking at Mona Lisa's hand, for instance, viewers can find no line where one finger ends and the next one begins; the separation is done totally with shadows. This unified vision of the world affected the content of his paintings as well as the technique. Background and subject often echo each other in a picture: the drapery and folds of the subject's clothing may reflect background scenes of curving vines or rocky hills or water that flows.

Leonardo recognized the great diversity surrounding him, but he believed that an even greater unity supported the diversity and his own work was an expression of that unity.

CHAPTER 22   **PART 4**

Misplaced and dangling modifiers

Exercise 22-a
Misplaced and dangling modifiers

To read about this topic, see the section on misplaced and dangling modifiers in your handbook.

Circle the letter of the more effective sentence in each pair. Example:

   a. **Karl Marx almost spent all of his time writing, using every waking moment to get his ideas down on paper.**

   (b.) **Karl Marx spent almost all of his time writing, using every waking moment to get his ideas down on paper.**

1. a. Between 1852 and 1862, Karl Marx just wrote more than three hundred articles for the *New York Tribune*.

    b. Between 1852 and 1862, Karl Marx wrote more than three hundred articles just for the *New York Tribune*.

2. a. During his lifetime, Marx did not receive much attention. But people all over the world paid attention to what he had written after his death.

    b. During his lifetime, Marx did not receive much attention. But after his death, people all over the world paid attention to what he had written.

3. a. He wanted only one thing for himself: recognition of the importance of his ideas.

    b. He only wanted one thing for himself: recognition of the importance of his ideas.

4. a. Capitalist scholars tend to usually say that Marx's work is "illogical" and "uninformed."

    b. Capitalist scholars usually tend to say that Marx's work is "illogical" and "uninformed."

5. a. However, most capitalists agree that as a student of social organization, he was brilliant.

    b. However, most capitalists agree that he, as a student of social organization, was brilliant.

Exercise 22-b
Misplaced and dangling modifiers

Name

Date   Section

To read about this topic, see the section on misplaced and dangling modifiers in your handbook.

Edit the following paragraphs to eliminate misplaced and dangling modifiers. The first revision has been done for you.

Karl Marx wrote *The Communist Manifesto*, his most famous work, in collaboration with Friedrich Engels just before the German revolution of 1848. The book has three sections with distinct characteristics.

In the first section, Marx tries to ~~accurately~~ define terms ^accurately and to state his basic assumptions. He traces the class systems of earlier times and concludes that there are only two classes in his day, the bourgeoisie and the proletariat. The bourgeoisie are the property-owning capitalists; the proletariat are the working class. Marx asserts that as the bourgeoisie increase their economic power, they work toward their own eventual downfall.

Set up in question-and-answer format, Marx made the second section of his *Communist Manifesto* resemble a debate with a bourgeois sympathizer. Of course, Marx only sees one side of the debate as being correct. After "defeating" his opponent on major questions, Marx presents his own ten-point program in clear, easy-to-understand, persuasive language.

Marx, after developing the second section in detail, moves on to the *Manifesto*'s final section. He shows how Communists and other reform groups work toward the same goals. Reminding workers that they "have nothing to lose but their chains," Marx calls on them to zealously and actively work together. Marx utters the slogan that can still be heard today in ringing tones: "Workers of the world, unite!"

CHAPTER 23

PART 4

Sentence variety

Exercise 23-a
Sentence variety

To read about this topic, see the section on sentence variety in your handbook.

Edit each of the following sentences in at least two ways, to provide varied openings and varied sentence structures. You may need to change other parts of each sentence as well. Example:

 a. ~~Martin Luther King Jr. was in~~ ⟨In⟩ jail awaiting a hearing⟨,⟩ ~~he~~ ⟨Martin Luther King Jr.⟩ read a newspaper article attacking his work.

 b. ⟨When⟩ Martin Luther King Jr. was in jail awaiting a hearing⟨,⟩ he read a newspaper article attacking his work.

1. a. King didn't have much to write on in the jail, so he started writing in the margins of the newspaper in which the article appeared.

   b. King didn't have much to write on in the jail, so he started writing in the margins of the newspaper in which the article appeared.

2. a. A black trusty, wanting to help King, was able to get some scraps of paper for him after a while.

   b. A black trusty, wanting to help King, was able to get some scraps of paper for him after a while.

3. a. His attorneys were later allowed to give him a pad of paper. King, fired up by the newspaper article, quickly filled the pad.

    b. His attorneys were later allowed to give him a pad of paper. King, fired up by the newspaper article, quickly filled the pad.

4. a. King chose to write his response to the newspaper article in letter form, so he seemed like the biblical Paul to some people.

    b. King chose to write his response to the newspaper article in letter form, so he seemed like the biblical Paul to some people.

5. a. How were King and Paul alike? Paul, a preacher of the Christian faith like King, wrote some of his famous letters from a prison cell.

    b. How were King and Paul alike? Paul, a preacher of the Christian faith like King, wrote some of his famous letters from a prison cell.

Name	
Date	Section

To read about this topic, see the section on sentence variety in your handbook.

The following paragraphs are grammatically correct but dull. Revise them to add variety. You may need to combine some sentences. The first revision has been done for you.

>   *After studying*
> Everyone has heard of Martin Luther King Jr. ~~He studied~~ for the ministry at Boston
>
>   *earning*
> University and ~~earned~~ a doctorate in theology, ~~and then~~ he went home to the South to
>
> work as a minister. He started working in civil rights and became the most influential
>
> leader of that cause in America. When he died, the victim of an assassin's bullet, his
>
> name was almost synonymous with "civil rights." Historians and biographers have
>
> recorded his leadership in the fight to gain basic civil rights for all Americans. Many
>
> people who know of his civil rights work, however, are not aware of his skill as a
>
> writer. King produced other important writing in addition to his carefully crafted and
>
> emotional speeches.
>
>   King's "Letter from Birmingham Jail" is among his most famous writings. He
>
> wrote it to answer a statement published by eight Alabama ministers that King's
>
> work was "unwise and untimely," and the letter shows King to be a man who had
>
> great patience with his critics. King is eager to get these ministers to accept his point
>
> of view, so he reminds them that they are ministers. Their goodwill, he says, should
>
> help them see that his views hold value. He does not attack them personally. He
>
> analyzes their arguments. Then he presents his own views. Does he use many of the
>
> emotional appeals for which he is justly famous? No, in this letter King depends on
>
> logic and reasoning as the tools to win his argument.

CHAPTER 24

PART 4

Sentence fragments

Exercise 24-a
Sentence fragments

Name	
Date	Section

To read about this topic, see the section on fragments in your handbook.

Each of the following word groups includes a subordinating word. One word group in each pair contains a fragment. Write "OK" after each item that does not contain a fragment and write "frag" after each item that contains a fragment. Example:

   a. **John Lennon lived with his Aunt Mimi until he was grown. Because his parents had separated and his mother had given John to Mimi.** *frag*

   b. **His father took him from Mimi when John was about five. Because his mother returned him to Mimi, he grew up as Mimi's child.** *OK*

1.   a. When John Lennon was a teenager, his mother, Julia, began to pay more attention to his interests. _____

    b. When Julia, John Lennon's mother, bought him a guitar and let him stay with her instead of his Aunt Mimi. _____

2.   a. Although he studied art in college, he soon became more interested in music. _____

    b. Although Julia encouraged his music and put up with the boyish pranks that annoyed Aunt Mimi. _____

3.   a. His mother died before he was an adult. While John was still in college, in fact. _____

    b. Mimi's husband, his uncle, had died while John still lived with them. _____

4.   a. John asked Paul McCartney to join his group, and later Paul brought in George Harrison, and all three asked Ringo Starr to join them. Before they cut their first record. _____

b. In their early days, the Beatles copied people like Elvis Presley and Little Richard. Before these English boys even visited America, they sang with American accents. _____

5. a. The Beatles gave one reason for quitting their tours in 1966. That the tours were wrecking their playing. _____

   b. Stopping the tours gave the Beatles an opportunity to expand their talents. That they learned to read musical notes and write their own music was key to their improvement as musicians. _____

Exercise 24-b
Sentence fragments

To read about this topic, see the section on fragments in your handbook.

Edit the following paragraphs to eliminate sentence fragments. The first revision has been done for you.

Four
~~How four~~ young Englishmen added a word to the world's vocabulary in the 1960s. A word that became synonymous with the 1960s. Especially with the music of that time. That word was, of course, "Beatles." The Beatles became the most famous popular musical group of the twentieth century. And have held the loyalty of many fans into the present century.

The Beatles were popular in Liverpool, England, and in Hamburg, Germany. Before they came to America on tour and became world famous. Liverpool and Hamburg loved the four young men and their music. The Beatles' favorite club was the Cavern in Liverpool. Where they hung out together, played day and night, and attracted many fans. A Liverpool disc jockey first called attention to them, and a Liverpool music critic and record store owner became their first manager. The disc jockey called them "fantastic." Saying that they had "resurrected original rock 'n' roll." The music critic who became their manager, Brian Epstein, made them shape up as a group. Promoting them, arranging club dates for them, and badgering record companies for them. He was determined to win a recording contract for this exciting new group.

In England, the record buying led to the publicity. In America, the publicity led to the record buying. Everyone wanted copies of the original singles. "Love Me Do," "Please Please Me," and "From Me to You." In America, audiences made so much noise that no one could hear the music. Crowds of screaming teenagers surrounded the Beatles wherever they went. Determined to touch one or more of these famous music makers. Reporters observing the conduct of fans at Beatles' concerts found that they had to invent a new word. To describe the wild, almost insane behavior of the fans. They called it "Beatlemania."

CHAPTER 25

Run-on sentences

Exercise 25-a
Run-on sentences

Name		
Date		Section

To read about this topic, see the section on run-on sentences in your handbook.

One sentence in each of the following pairs is a run-on sentence. Find and correct the error, using an effective revision strategy. Mark the correct sentence "OK." Example:

      Although

a. Joe Hill may not have been the first martyr of the labor movement, ~~however,~~ he was certainly its most skillful worker with words and music.

b. Before his arrest in 1914 for killing a grocer in Salt Lake City, Joe Hill was simply the Swedish immigrant Joseph Hillstrom; no one knew or cared much about him. *OK*

1. a. Ralph Chaplin was the only person who wrote anything about Joe Hill before Hill's execution, he jotted down just a few notes based on an interview with a drunken sailor.

   b. Extensive historical research has not confirmed or denied those notes because researchers have turned up quite different stories.

2. a. All the evidence introduced at Hill's trial was circumstantial; furthermore, the dead man's son, who had witnessed the murder, refused to identify Hill as the gunman.

   b. Did the state hide evidence it certainly seemed that way.

3. a. One Wobbly told the police that he had been with Joe Hill in another location on the night of the murder, he also told a detective he could prove Hill's innocence.

   b. That man was promptly arrested and held in jail for the duration of the trial.

4. a. At the end of the trial, the man was released and ordered to leave the state.

    b. Hill's own attorneys did not do much to help him their attitude was as negative as that of the prosecutors.

5. a. Because of their negative attitude, Hill discharged both of the attorneys who were supposed to be defending him.

    b. "I have three prosecutors here, I intend to get rid of two of them," he said.

6. a. The state never showed a motive for the murder; furthermore, much evidence that Hill's attorneys could have used was never introduced.

    b. How did Hill get that bullet wound in his chest, he told the doctor he had gotten it in a fight over a woman.

7. a. The doctor who treated Hill was not asked to testify about medical aspects of the case, as a matter of fact, his testimony probably would have prevented Hill's conviction.

    b. Protests about Hill's conviction came from all over the world, but they were ignored.

8. a. Important political figures tried to help Hill, hoping until the last minute that they could save him.

    b. The Swedish consul pleaded for him, President Wilson sent telegrams to the governor of Utah.

9. a. Legend has it that Hill's last words before the firing squad were "Don't mourn for me; organize," in fact, he said, "Yes, aim! Let her go! Fire!"

    b. If Joe Hill is known at all today, it is probably because of Joe Glazer, his guitar, and the song "Joe Hill."

10. a. Glazer was not the composer of "Joe Hill" its composers were Earl Robinson and Alfred Hayes.

    b. Glazer, however, made the song known across America, singing it at banquets as well as on picket lines.

Exercise 25-b
Run-on sentences

To read about this topic, see the section on run-on sentences in your handbook.

Revise each run-on sentence in the following paragraphs. The first sentence has been revised for you.

Although he
~~He~~ never calls them by name, John Steinbeck immortalizes the Wobblies in *The Grapes of Wrath*. The novel is about the life of the Joad family. The Joads have lost their farm during the Depression, the family has come to California seeking work. There is no permanent work for anyone, moreover, the money earned by picking crops is not enough to feed the family.

Union organizers have talked to the workers about organizing and striking. Tom, the oldest Joad son, has listened to them, however, he has not yet joined them. Tom is in hiding because he has accidentally killed a man in a fight. He spends all his daylight hours alone, he has lots of time to think about his family's situation. Tom becomes convinced that life is unfair for his people, he decides to leave the family, find the union men, and work with them.

Tom is inarticulate when he tries to explain to Ma what he hopes to do he gropes for words to express his frustration and his hope. Ma asks him how she will know about him, she worries that he might get killed and she would not know. Tom's reassurances are almost mystical: "Wherever they's a fight so hungry people can eat, I'll be there. . . . An' when our folks eat the stuff they raise an' live in the houses they build — why, I'll be there."

If Tom had had a copy of the Wobblies' "little red song book," he could have found less mystical words. Every copy of the book contained the Wobblies' Preamble, the first sentence in the Preamble was unmistakably clear "The working class and the employing class have nothing in common." Tom would have understood those words he would have believed them, too.

CHAPTER 26

PART 4

Subject-verb agreement

Exercise 26-a
Subject-verb agreement

Name	
Date	Section

To read about this topic, see the section on subject-verb agreement in your handbook.

Each of the following sentences has two subjects and verbs (some of the subject-verb pairs are in subordinate structures). The simple subjects are italicized. Edit each incorrect verb to make it agree with its subject. Keep all verbs in the present tense. One subject-verb pair in each sentence is correct. Example:

> "*Sour grapes*" ~~are~~ is a common expression, but not *everyone* knows the origin of that phrase.

1. Aesop's *story* "The Fox and the Grapes" tells about a fox *who* try unsuccessfully to get some grapes.

2. There are a big *bunch* of grapes hanging over the top of a wall, and the *fox* is hot and thirsty.

3. A favorite *food* of his are grapes, and *he* leaps up to get some — without success.

4. Hoping that no *crowd* of friends are watching, the *fox* takes a running leap for the top of the wall.

5. Unsuccessful, the *fox* in the story tries again and again with the same result; neither his *cleverness* nor his high *leaps* is successful.

6. Embarrassed, the *fox* fears that *news* of his failures are going to give his friends something to tease him about.

7. The fox's *pride* and his *self-confidence* has suffered, so *he* claims not to want the grapes anyway.

8. The *fox*, stalking proudly off with his nose in the air, say that the *grapes* are sour.

9. *Everyone* know that the *fox* does not believe his own words.

10. To save their pride, *people* often pretends not to want what *they* cannot get.

To read about this topic, see the section on subject-verb agreement in your handbook.

Choose the correct verb from each pair in parentheses and circle it. The first selection has been made for you.

From one of Aesop's lesser-known fables (comes / come) the question "Who's going to bell the cat?" The fable "Belling the Cat" describes the long battle between mice and cats.

In the story, a committee of mice is appointed to find a way to keep the cat from killing so many mice. Everyone on the committee (tries / try) to solve the problem. There (is / are) many committee meetings and much discussion, but in the end neither the committee nor its chairperson (is / are) able to make any good suggestions. Finally, the time comes for the committee to make its report at a public meeting. Embarrassed, the committee (reports / report) its failure.

At first, there is only silence; no one wants to accept the committee's report as the final word on the problem. Then a little pip-squeak among the mice (suggests / suggest) tying a bell on the cat. The young mouse makes quite a speech in favor of his idea. According to that mouse, statistics (shows / show) that no mice have ever been captured by a noisy cat. The mouse points out that his solution would not cost much; a bell and a string (is / are) all the equipment needed to give the mice warning of the cat's approach. The mouse who makes the suggestion gets a round of applause. The committee members, who (wishes / wish) that they had thought of the idea, are silent. Then a wise old mouse asks, "Who will bell the cat?" The experienced mice and the young pip-squeak (is / are) silent.

It is easy to make suggestions that other people (has / have) to carry out.

CHAPTER 27

PART 4

Pronoun reference

Exercise 27-a
Pronoun reference

Name	
Date	Section

To read about this topic, see the section on pronoun reference in your handbook.

Six of the following sentences contain faulty pronoun references. Find the faulty references and fix them. Mark the correct sentences "OK." Example:

> Mary Jones, who came to be known as "Mother" Jones, got a job working in the textile
> *and this job*
> mills, ~~which~~ made her conscious of how women workers were mistreated.
>   ^

1. When Mother Jones started working in the textile mills at the turn of the twentieth century, she saw "the little gray ghosts," the child laborers which worked from sunup to sundown.

2. Children as young as six scooted along the floor oiling and cleaning the huge whirring looms, which often devoured a child's fingers or hand.

3. Mother Jones once led a delegation of three hundred children from Philadelphia to New York to dramatize their plight; in some of the newspapers, they called her "the greatest female agitator in the country."

4. The speeches Mother Jones made about child labor were among her best: They called for legislation to forbid labor practices dangerous to children's health.

5. When Mother Jones asked for permission to bring three of the children to meet with President Theodore Roosevelt in New York, she was refused. It saddened her because she had hoped for the president's help.

6.   Mother Jones asked again and was again refused. This second one saddened her even more, but she still did not consider the trip a failure.

7.   She told the children and their parents that they had been successful.

8.   Public awareness, which she felt would help the children, gradually began to increase.

9.   Thousands of people had learned about the children's plight, which was bound to affect their thinking about child labor laws.

10. Mother Jones's optimism had another basis as well: The children would remember—and they would grow up.

Exercise 27-b
Pronoun reference

To read about this topic, see the section on pronoun reference in your handbook.

Edit the following paragraphs to correct errors in pronoun reference. The first revision has been done for you.

Coal miners' struggles turned into actual war in the Kanawha Valley of West Virginia, where ~~they~~ miners were striking. The mine owners dominated the courts and the newspapers; they did not need to worry about the law or public opinion. Although the miners did not want to accept this, they were often forced to face it. Guards used violent tactics to maintain the mine owners' control, once spraying strikers' tent colonies with machine-gun fire and kicking a pregnant woman so hard that her unborn child died in the womb.

Mary "Mother" Jones urged the miners to fight while she tried to gain the ear of the governor, federal lawmakers, and the public. In records of the fight, it says that two thousand miners came from outside the valley to help in the battle. The state militia was called in, but the owners got control of the militia soon after it arrived. En route to the state legislature to ask them for help, Mother Jones was kidnapped by soldiers, held incommunicado, put in solitary confinement, and tried by a military court. When the new governor of West Virginia, Henry D. Hatfield, investigated, he found a soldier guarding an eighty-year-old pneumonia-ridden woman that had a 104-degree fever.

Word about the Kanawha situation got out, but Governor Hatfield acted first. Out of his work came the Hatfield Agreement. This document, which historians of the labor movement consider a major advance for workers in the United States, forced the companies to recognize the union and to shorten the workday. Even more important, it stipulated that companies must pay wages in US currency. He also guaranteed civilians the right to civil, not military, trials and dismissed all sentences the military court had imposed—including the twenty-year prison term it had set for Mother Jones.

CHAPTER 28

PART 4

Pronoun and noun case

Exercise 28-a

Pronoun and noun case

Name	
Date	Section

To read about this topic, see the section on pronoun and noun case in your handbook.

Six of the following sentences have errors in pronoun or noun case. Find and fix the errors. Mark "OK" next to the sentences that have no errors. Example:

> **Mary "Mother" Jones liked to discuss union affairs with her friend Terence Powderly;**
>
> **she and ~~him~~ could argue for hours about the best approach to a problem.**
>   *he*

1. People all over the world knew about Mother Jones. Wherever she went, she was invited into their homes and their workplaces.

2. Once when she was traveling with Fred Mooney in Mexico, a crowd stopped the train and urged Mooney and she to open the train window.

3. Mooney and she were not sure whether they should open the window, but they decided to do so. When they did, she and him both were showered with red carnations and blue violets.

4. Although the people gave the flowers to both him and her, the flowers were meant as gifts in honor of "Madre Yones," as the people called her.

5. The trip to Mexico was exhausting, but it was she, over ninety years old, who never ran out of energy.

6. When Mooney fretted about her health, it was her who laughed and proposed that they get on with their sightseeing.

7. No one was more excited than her about the idea of a Pan-American Federation of Labor, an organization that would unite workers from Canada to South America.

8. The president of Mexico was as pleased as her at the idea of bringing together all the working people in the hemisphere.

9. "This is the beginning of a new day for us working people," exclaimed Mother Jones.

10. It was a day Mother Jones long remembered; years later it brought happy smiles to she and her friends whenever they saw carnations and violets or thought of that day's events.

To read about this topic, see the section on pronoun and noun case in your handbook.

Some of the personal pronouns in this passage are italicized; six of them are not in the correct case. The first one has been corrected for you. Find and correct the other five.

          Though *her* [she] and a friend would occasionally work together on the friend's campaign, Mother Jones avoided politics most of the time. *She*, the agitator, had no more interest in politics and political science than *her*, the labor organizer, had in economic theory. Mother Jones understood one kind of economics, the kind that dealt with wages, benefits, and the cost of bread and housing. The here-and-now problems of the poor called to Mother Jones so strongly that *she* had to do what *she* could to stop the injustice she saw around *her*.

          Surprisingly, Mother Jones was not a supporter of women's suffrage. When the fight to win women's right to vote came along, it was not *her* who supported it. *Herself* and her people were the working classes, both men and women, and neither *she* nor *them* had much patience for the "society women" who led the movement. As far as Mother Jones was concerned, well-dressed women parading down the city streets carrying placards and banners did not help working men and women obtain a decent life. Mother Jones objected to *them* spending time and energy and money on activities that would not help her kind of people. Nor was *she* interested in helping a cause that would benefit only women; her concern was for all workers, regardless of gender. *She* seemed not to understand that the votes of the miners' wives might do as much to help the working men as *her* agitating and organizing did.

CHAPTER 29

Verbs

Exercise 29-a
Verbs

Name	
Date	Section

To read about this topic, see the sections on verb forms in your handbook.

Edit the following paragraphs for missing *-ed* endings and incorrect forms of irregular verbs. The first revision has been done for you. You should make ten more.

          led
    Women who ~~leaded~~ the suffrage movement never used violence, but they thought

of themselves as waging a war. They tried different strategies in different places and

coordinated their various attacks. Some concentrated on state and local voting rights

for women; others work for national suffrage. In Washington, DC, they picketed,

demonstrated, and builded and maintained "perpetual watchfires" in which they

burned the speeches on democracy that President Wilson was giving in Europe.

    When the protesters were arrested at the White House in 1917, police had to

use their personal cars to carry the many prisoners they arrest. After the women

and some of their supporters were tried and found guilty, the judge got so tired of

sentencing them that when he reached twenty-six, he dismiss all the others.

    The women's organizing and demonstrating finally paid off. On May 21, 1919, the

House of Representatives passed the Nineteenth Amendment, giving women the right

to vote, and sended it to the Senate. On June 4, the Senate approved it and passed it

along to the states for ratification.

Women's groups kept up the pressure on the states during the long, tense ratification process. When, after more than a year, thirty-five states had ratified the amendment, it all come down to one man's vote in Tennessee. Whom do history remember as the hero of ratification? It was a young legislator named Harry Burn, who cast the tie-breaking vote. On August 24, the governor of Tennessee certified the vote and sent the results to Washington.

The US secretary of state had tell his staff to wake him as soon as the certificate arrived. He wanted to avoid a formal signing in the presence of the campaigning women. Nevertheless, on August 26, 1920, more than seventy years after women had first began to organize for suffrage, it was now official: Women in the United States had the right to vote.

To read about this topic, see the sections on verb forms in your handbook.

Edit the following paragraphs to correct problems with -s and -ed verb forms. The first revision has been done for you. You should make ten more.

Many historians ~~has~~ *have* agreed that the woman suffrage movement in the United States is rooted in the Seneca Falls Convention of 1848. The convention was organize by Elizabeth Cady Stanton and Lucretia Mott, after Mott was denied a seat as a delegate at an antislavery convention in London.

The Seneca Falls Convention is best known for a document produce by Stanton called the Declaration of Sentiments. Stanton's declaration remain one of the most important documents in American women's history. Modeled on the Declaration of Independence (1776), the Declaration of Sentiments list eighteen grievances—but these are grievances of women against their treatment by men and male-dominated society. Stanton's declaration explicitly state that "all men and women are created equal" and that women "demand the equal station to which they are entitled."

A modern reader don't have to read more than a few sentences of each document to see the similarities between the two. In fact, it have been said that the Declaration of Sentiments might have been rejected if its format hadn't seemed so familiar to those who attended the convention. The Declaration of Independence demand that men in America, like men in England, be represented in government. The Declaration of Sentiments argue that women, like men, should be represented in government. The women's document go so far as to suggest that American women should have the right to vote. In 1848, this idea was shocking—so shocking that it would take seventy-two years for women's right to vote to become a reality.

Name

Date | Section

To read about this topic, see the sections on verb forms in your handbook.

Use the tense indicated at the end of each sentence to write the correct form of the verb in brackets. Example:

People from many countries ___*entered*___ **[enter] the United States in the 1980s.**

[Past]

1. Eighty percent of the immigrants who _____ [*migrate*] to the United States in the 1980s were Asian or Latin American. [Past]

2. The number of Asians who _____ [*live*] in the United States more than doubled between 1970 and 1980. [Past progressive]

3. People from the Philippines, China, and Korea _____ [*be*] regular immigrants to the United States. [Present perfect]

4. Since 1975, a rush of immigrant refugees _____ [*arrive*] in the United States. [Present perfect progressive]

5. In less than a seven-year period, 600,000 refugees from Vietnam, Laos, and Cambodia _____ [*come*] to the United States. [Past]

CHAPTER 30

Articles

PART 4

Exercise 30-a
Articles

Name	
Date	Section

To read about this topic, see the section on articles in your handbook.

Some of the following sentences contain errors in the use of articles. Mark the correct sentences "OK" and correct the others. Example:

> Rhodopis charmed the animals: birds, monkeys, and even ~~an~~ ^{*a*} hippopotamus would
>
> do what she asked.

1. The animals loved to watch her dance; her tiny feet seemed never to touch path.

2. One night when her owner saw her dancing, he was enchanted and decided that such feet deserved special shoes.

3. Rhodopis's shoes had the leather soles, but the toes had a gold on them.

4. When Rhodopis danced, shoes sparkled; they seemed alive.

5. Jealous, the servant girls gave her the more chores; by nighttime, Rhodopis was almost too tired for a single dance.

6. Pharaoh, the ruler of Egypt, sent out a invitation for all his subjects to appear at a court festival.

7. Everyone wanted to go to festival; Rhodopis looked forward to dancing there.

8. The other girls gave her extra chores so that she would not be able to get away: washing the clothes, grinding the grain, and planting the garden.

9. While Rhodopis was doing a laundry, a hippopotamus splashed into the water.

10. The splash muddied Rhodopis's shoes; she cleaned the shoes and set them high on the riverbank to keep them safe.

To read about this topic, see the section on articles in your handbook.

Edit the following paragraphs to correct the use of articles. The first revision has been done for you.

People all over the world have stories that are part of their culture. Many cultures have ^a^ creation story that explains how the world came to be. Sometimes story tells how a single piece of the world got its characteristics. It is not surprising that these stories exist; what is surprising is how similar the stories are. Consider Cinderella story, for example. Cinderella has different names in different places, and details of her adventure are not the same; but the basic story echoes around a world.

In the Egypt, she is called Rhodopis (the word means "rosy cheeked"). Rhodopis is a Greek slave in a Egyptian home. She does not have eyes or an hair like anyone else in the home. Her green eyes look quite different from eyes of the other girls. Their dark, straight hair almost never gets tangled; her yellow, curly hair blows into tangled mass around her face. Her light-skinned face turns red and burns when she is in sun too long. When someone calls her "Rosy Rhodopis," she blushes, and her cheeks become rosier.

Unable to make the friends with the other girls, Rhodopis turns to the animals in the nearby woods and streams for companionship.

CHAPTER 31

Commas and unnecessary commas

Exercise 31-a
Commas and unnecessary commas

Name	
Date	Section

To read about this topic, see the sections on the comma in your handbook.

Insert commas where they are needed and delete commas where they are not needed. If a sentence is correct, mark it "OK." Example:

> **The lack of complacency in the dystopian novel can be seen on the first page, often in the first paragraph.**

1. One of the earliest contributors to the young adult dystopian genre is Lois Lowry whose novel *The Giver* won the Newbery Medal in 1994. [Lowry wrote more than one novel.]

2. *The Giver* is still taught in schools alongside the older dystopian novels, *Brave New World* and *Animal Farm*.

3. *The Giver*, which has continued to appeal to young readers, caused quite a stir when it was published because of its troublesome subject matter.

4. Parents of adolescents at the time thumbed through *The Giver* with trepidation a feeling with which many readers approached the book.

5. *The Giver*'s story and its immense popularity still resonate today; in April 2012, the Minnesota Opera, based in Minneapolis, presented Susan Kander's operatic vision of *The Giver* to sold-out shows.

6. Jonas the protagonist is given the role of receiver of memories.

7.   As Jonas accepts memories from the current receiver, a wise old man known as the Giver he experiences love, loss, color, the sun, snow, terror, and excitement for the first time.

8.   When the Giver tells Jonas the true meaning of the ceremony known as "release" the two decide to join forces to save their community.

9.   To give the memories of the past back to the community Jonas must escape to Elsewhere and leave the Giver behind to help people cope with the flood of emotion and changes to come.

10.   Although subject matter such as this can be challenging for young readers, Lowry has said "Pretending that there are no choices to be made—reading only books, for example, which are cheery and safe and nice—is a prescription for disaster for the young."

Name	
Date	Section

To read about this topic, see the sections on unnecessary commas in your handbook.

One sentence in each of the following pairs is correctly punctuated. Circle the letter of the correct sentence and edit the incorrect sentence. Example:

(a.) Writers of young adult dystopian literature depict heroes and heroines who, while flawed and imperfect, possess the morals and the tenacity of the best role models.

b. Though these characters make mistakes and break rules, their motives and their determination/ are a reflection of their desire to do good.

1. a. Their audacity, which we see in Katniss in *The Hunger Games*, reflects the individuality, and self-assertion portrayed in more and more young female protagonists.

   b. Increasingly in young adult fiction, the love interest story line is subordinate to the heroine's moral dilemma.

2. a. Dystopian works tend to be less angst-filled and romanticized than other young adult works like, the Twilight series.

   b. Despite being desperately in love, most protagonists don't dwell on appearances or emotions because they're too busy trying to save the world.

3. a. Scott Westerfield's Uglies series imagines a postapocalyptic world in which all teenagers are ugly, until radical surgery at age sixteen makes them into supermodel "pretties."

   b. Published in 2005, Westerfield's first novel, *Uglies*, was admired by girls and young women because it allowed them to talk about the pressure they felt about their looks, an age-old anxiety.

4. a. The author's depiction of the consequences that can arise from body alteration for the sake of beauty gives the book plenty of complex topics for readers to consider.

    b. The fact that *Uglies* and the books that followed it were wildly popular, proves that girls and young women want to read about challenging topics that they can relate to.

5. a. When teenagers can talk about the pressure to conform to a standard of beauty, they have a better chance of accepting themselves as they are.

    b. The dystopian novel, like its science fiction counterpart, has the power to examine, and change the way our society functions.

Commas and unnecessary commas

Name	
Date	Section

To read about this topic, see the sections on commas and unnecessary commas in your handbook.

Edit the following essay by adding commas where they are needed and removing unnecessary commas. The first revision has been done for you.

Young adult dystopian literature is a popular genre with a growing fan base worldwide; its books are characterized by degradation, totalitarian states, and dehumanization. With the release of the film version of Suzanne Collins's *The Hunger Games*͵ the genre has amassed a following similar to that of wizards and vampires in fiction and pop culture. Writers such as Lois Lowry and M. T. Anderson have been producing award-winning dystopian work for years. But the wild popularity of such writers reveals that young readers welcome the serious dark work being marketed to them. The dystopian novel takes risks and teenagers like risks. In sophisticated ways that are satisfying to young readers, these books depict pain, loss, and the anxieties of growing up.

Dystopia is the opposite of utopia which is any system of political or social perfection an ideal place or state. Dystopia signifies regression. It is a fictional society characterized by, poverty, oppression, disease, or overcrowding. The world in a dystopian novel is recognizable as a warped version of our own; people may survive an epic tragedy, often environmental or political, and survivors form a society, that curtails freedoms to protect citizens. A hero or heroine must triumph over terrible odds to better the society, and restore harmony. The novels are often violent. While the violence may disturb parents teenagers want stories with weight and intensity. They want to immerse themselves in a world where there is no happy ending, a world that challenges and shocks them and where they can see the best and the worst of humanity.

## CHAPTER 32

Apostrophes

Exercise 32-a
Apostrophes

Name	
Date	Section

To read about this topic, see the section on the apostrophe in your handbook.

Each of the following sentences has two words containing apostrophes. Only one of the apostrophes is used correctly in each sentence. Delete or move the other apostrophe. Example:

> **Further back in American history, one woman's soldiering had made her famous; no**
>
> **one has yet had a story to match ~~her's~~.** *hers*

1. Deborah Sampson never dreamed that she would someday fight in battles' for American independence, much less that the battles' outcomes might depend on her.

2. Because her parents' income was not enough to support their children, her parents' sent Deborah to live with relatives in another town.

3. Later she was sent to live in a foster family with ten sons'; the sons' acceptance of her was wholehearted, and one son became her fiancé when she grew up.

4. The Revolutionary War was'nt over when news of his death reached Deborah; she wasn't long in making a major decision.

5. Determined that his place should become her's, she enlisted under a man's name.

Exercise 32-b
Apostrophes

Name

Date | Section

To read about this topic, see the section on the apostrophe in your handbook.

The following sentences contain no apostrophes. Add any that are needed and make any necessary corrections in spelling. If a sentence is correct, mark it "OK." Example:

> Who's   who's
> ~~Whose~~ to say ~~whos~~ right about Deborah Sampson's decision?
>   ^   ^

1. If men have the right to fight for their beliefs, should women have the right to fight for theirs?

2. Its clear that Deborah Sampson thought so; she enlisted twice to fight for hers.

3. On her first attempt, Sampson enlisted almost at the end of the day—and was discovered before its end arrived.

4. Though drinking was not a habit of hers, she spent her first evening as a soldier copying other new soldiers behavior.

5. Coming to the aid of this very noisy, very drunk, and very sick "buddy" of theirs, they soon were asking, "Whose this?"

Exercise 32-c
Apostrophes

Name

Date | Section

To read about this topic, see the section on the apostrophe in your handbook.

In the following paragraphs, add apostrophes where they are missing and delete or correct them where they are misused. The first revision has been done for you.

During the 1990 troubles in Panama, American television and newspaper reporters had an exciting piece of news. They reported that for the first time American female soldiers had been engaged in actual combat. Acting as her ~~soldiers~~ soldiers' leader, Captain Linda Bray led her troops into combat. Names of two additional women who were involved in combat, Staff Sergeant April Hanley and Private First Class Christina Proctor, were reported in the newspapers. Their's were the only names reported, although other women also took part in the fighting.

It wasn't the first time an American woman had fought in an American battle, but its not likely that many people are aware of that fact. The Civil War had its female fighters too. Loreta Janeta Velazquez fought for the Confederates' in the Civil War after her husbands death. Like many other women whose husbands were killed in that war, she must have asked herself, "Whose going to take his place in battle?" The decision to fight was her's alone. Someone is sure to ask how that was possible, especially in those days. Military identification was not very sophisticated in the 1860s. Someones willingness to fight was that person's major qualification, and each fighting unit needed to replace it's losses as fast as possible. Velazquez simply disguised herself in mens clothing, found a troop needing replacements, and joined the fight. Loreta Janeta Velazquez was Linda Brays Civil War predecessor.

CHAPTER 33

PART 4

Quotation marks

Exercise 33-a
Quotation marks

Name	
Date	Section

To read about this topic, see the section on quotation marks in your handbook.

Edit the following sentences to correct the use of quotation marks and of punctuation with quotation marks. Example:

> **The parents watched as the doctor bandaged the boy's eyes. "For the love of**
>
> **God, what can we do?" asked the father⸮.**
>   ^   ^

1. The doctor answered "You can do nothing but pray."

2. When the bandages were removed and the shades were opened to let in the bright sunlight, the doctor asked, "What do you see"?

3. "Nothing," said the boy. I see nothing.

4. The village priest said "I have recently seen a remarkable school." He had just returned from a trip to Paris.

5. "In this school, he added blind students are taught to read."

6. "You didn't say "read," did you?" asked the boy's father.

7. The boy responded to the priest's words as if they were a trick of some kind "Now you are joking with me. How can such a thing be possible?"

8. The boy, Louis, thought it would be great fun to "visit" that school someday.

9. His father promised "We will go soon, Louis."

10. And so it happened that ten-year-old Louis Braille entered the National Institute for Blind Youth and began the long effort to erase the fear people had of even the word blind.

To read about this topic, see the section on quotation marks in your handbook.

Edit the following paragraphs to correct the use of quotation marks and of punctuation used with quotation marks. The first correction has been made for you.

Louis Braille entered the National Institute for Blind Youth in Paris when he was ten. At twelve, he was already experimenting with a system of raised dots on paper known as "night-~~writing~~", *writing,"* which was used by the military. Institute teachers decided that night-writing was impractical, but Louis became proficient at it. When Charles Barbier, inventor of the system, visited the institute, Louis told him "Your symbols are too large and too complicated. Impressed, Barbier encouraged him and said that "since Louis was blind himself, he might discover the magic key that had eluded his teachers."

Louis Braille wanted a system that could transcribe everything from a textbook on science to a poem like Heinrich Heine's Loreley. At fifteen, he had worked out his own system of six dots arranged in various patterns. "Read to me," he said to one of his teachers, and I will take down your words." As the teacher read, Louis punched dots onto his paper and then read the passage back without error. The teacher exclaimed, "Remarkable"! Government officials, not impressed enough to take any action, said simply that Braille should be encouraged. "You didn't say "encouraged," did you?" asked Braille. He wanted official acceptance, not simply encouragement. "The system has proved itself," said Louis. We have been using it for five years now."

For most people, the word Braille itself now means simply a system of reading and writing used by blind people; for blind people, it means freedom and independence. Braille himself died before his system was recognized beyond the institute. The plaque on the house of his birth, however, records the world's recognition of his work with these words: He opened the doors of knowledge to all those who cannot see.

Answers to exercises

Exercise 14-a, page 123 *Possible answers:*

1. An analysis of superhero films focused on male characters, with parenting as a theme. Possible audience is superhero film enthusiasts or film study scholars.
2. A cause-and-effect look at how reports of animal disease in news outlets affect consumer demand for meat products. Audience is probably a general audience.
3. An informative article aimed at experts—counselors who work in a school setting and see students who harm themselves or are thinking about doing so.

Exercise 14-b, page 124

1. Illustration. A general statement about black officials' responses to black crime is followed by examples of different responses.
2. Comparison and contrast. The writer compares and contrasts the responsibilities of two government agencies that regulate dietary supplements.

Exercise 14-c, page 126 *Possible answer:*

Modicum means small amount. The clue is the phrase "low-cost, low-effort" earlier in the sentence.

Exercise 14-d, page 127

Answers will vary.

Exercise 14-e, page 129

Answers will vary.

Exercise 14-f, page 131

Answers will vary.

Exercise 15-a, page 133

1. b; a is a question.
2. b; a is a fact and not debatable.
3. a; b is a fact and not debatable.
4. a; b is a fact and not debatable.
5. a; b is too general for a college paper.
6. a; b is too vague for an argument.
7. b; a is too general for a college paper.
8. a; b is both too general and too factual.

Exercise 15-b, page 136 *Possible answer:*

Investing in digital health monitoring is the best way for today's health care providers to promote patients' well-being and confidence in caregivers and, at the same time, lower their own costs in the long run.

Exercise 15-c, page 138

Answers will vary.

Exercise 16-a, page 142

1. a
2. c

Exercise 16-b, page 144 *Possible answers:*

1. Taking a mid-day nap can have benefits unrecognized by many people.
2. Afghan girls still face many obstacles to attending school, despite work by education advocates.

Exercise 16-c, page 145

Answer will vary.

Exercise 17-a, page 147

1. Plagiarized. The student uses some exact words and phrases from the source (*intimate, broken into discrete bits*) without enclosing them in quotation marks and also mimics the structure of the source.
2. OK. The student has correctly enclosed the exact words of the source in quotation marks and has used brackets for a word added to fit the surrounding sentence.
3. OK. The student has correctly enclosed the exact words of the source in quotation marks.
4. OK. The student has correctly paraphrased the source without using the language or structure of the source.
5. Plagiarized. The student has put quotation marks around exact words from the source but has failed to cite the author of the source in a signal phrase or in parentheses.

Exercise 17-b, page 149

1. Plagiarized. The student uses some exact words and phrases from the source (*spend more time thinking and talking about other people than . . . anything else*) without enclosing them in quotation marks and also mimics the structure of the source. The student also has not cited the source in a signal phrase or in parentheses.
2. OK. The student has correctly enclosed the exact words of the source in quotation marks and has cited the source of the quotation in parentheses.
3. OK. The student has correctly enclosed the exact words of the source in quotation marks and has cited the source of the quotations in a signal phrase and in parentheses.
4. Plagiarized. The student has put exact words from the source in quotation marks but has omitted the words *briefly but* after *themselves*, and that omission distorts the meaning of the source.
5. OK. The student has paraphrased the source's ideas without using the exact words or structure of the source and has cited the source in a signal phrase and in parentheses.

Exercise 17-c, page 151

1. Common knowledge. Yoknapatawpha County is mentioned in virtually all sources discussing Faulkner, so his invention of this place can be considered common knowledge.
2. Needs citation. The scholar whose research led to this hypothesis should be given credit.
3. Common knowledge. Information about birth and death dates and the life circumstances of well-known authors usually does not require citation.
4. Needs citation. A reader would not encounter this information repeatedly in books and articles on Shakespeare, so it requires a citation.
5. Needs citation. This information might be considered controversial, especially among admirers of Disney.
6. Common knowledge. This is information that would appear in many sources on Wordsworth and Shelley, so a paper on these poets would not need to cite it.
7. Needs citation. Statistics generally require a citation.
8. Common knowledge. This is a definition of a standard literary form—a type of information found in almost any introductory literature text.
9. Common knowledge. This information about Iris Murdoch is widely known, and a student would find mention of it in most recent sources related to Murdoch.
10. Needs citation. This information would probably be surprising to many readers (and some might doubt its truthfulness), so a citation is needed.

Exercise 17-d, page 153

1. This sentence is unacceptable. The second part of the sentence is a direct quotation from the source, so it must appear in quotation marks:

   Wind power accounts for more than 1% of California's electricity, reports Frederic Golden, and "[d]uring breezy early mornings in summer, the contribution goes even higher" (B1).
2. OK. Quoted words appear in quotation marks, and the student provides the author's name in the signal phrase and the page number in parentheses.
3. This sentence is unacceptable. The words appearing in quotation marks are not word-for-word accurate. Also, the statement is not accurate because the 8% figure applies only

on certain days. The following is an acceptable revision:

Mary A. Ilyin reports that under certain weather conditions, "the wind accounts for up to 8%" of California's electricity (qtd. in Golden B1).

4. OK. The brackets indicate that the word *California's* does not appear in the original source, and otherwise the quotation is word-for-word accurate. In addition, the MLA citation correctly indicates that the words belong to Ilyin, who was quoted by Golden.

5. This passage is unacceptable. The second sentence is a dropped quotation. Quotations should be introduced with a signal phrase, usually naming the author. The following is an acceptable revision:

California has pioneered the use of wind power. According to Frederic Golden, "Half of California's turbines . . . are located in Altamont Pass" (B1).

Exercise 17-e, page 155

1. OK. The student has put quotation marks around the exact words from the source and has handled the MLA citation correctly, putting the name of the author in a signal phrase and the page number in parentheses.

2. The sentence is unacceptable. The phrase *active safety* is enclosed in quotation marks in the source; single quotation marks are required for a quotation within a quotation. In addition, the student has failed to use an ellipsis mark to indicate that the word *which* is omitted from the quotation. The following is an acceptable revision:

Gladwell argues that "'active safety' . . . is every bit as important" as a vehicle's ability to withstand a collision (31).

3. This passage is unacceptable. The second sentence is a dropped quotation. Quotations should be introduced with a signal phrase, usually naming the author. The following is an acceptable revision:

A majority of drivers can, indeed, be wrong. As Malcolm Gladwell points out, "Most of us think that S.U.V.s are much safer than sports cars" (31).

4. OK. The student has introduced the quotation with a signal phrase and used brackets to indicate the change from *you* to *they* to fit the grammar of the sentence.

5. This sentence is unacceptable. The student has changed the wording of the source (*of surviving*) to fit the grammar of the sentence (*to survive*) but has not indicated the change with brackets. The following is an acceptable revision:

Gladwell explains that most people expect an SUV to survive "a collision with a hypothetical tractor-trailer in the other lane" (31).

Exercise 17-f, page 157

1. a. Because Sommers is quoted in an article written by someone else, MLA style requires the abbreviation "qtd. in" (for "quoted in") before the author of the article in the in-text citation.

2. b. When the author of a source is given in a signal phrase, the title of the source is not necessary in an in-text citation.

3. b. For a work with three or more authors, only the first author's name is used; "et al." is used in place of all other names.

4. a. Statistics taken from a source must be cited with author and page number.

5. b. The author's name, not the title of the source, should be used in an in-text citation.

6. a. The exact words of the source are enclosed in quotation marks.

7. b. For an unsigned source, a shortened form of the title is used in the in-text citation.

8. a. When the works cited list includes two or more works by one author, the in-text citation includes a shortened form of the title of the work cited.

9. b. A website with no author should be cited with a shortened form of the title, not with the sponsor of the website.

10. a. When a source has two authors, both authors should be named in the in-text citation.

Exercise 17-g, page 160

1. b. An MLA works cited entry for an article with no author begins with the title of the article.

2. b. The terms "volume" and "number" are abbreviated, and the name of the database and the URL for the database home page are included.

3. a. When citing a single work from an anthology, list the individual work first, beginning with its author's name.

4. b. If a newspaper article appears on pages that are not consecutive, the first page number is followed by a plus sign.
5. a. In an MLA works cited entry, the publication date appears after the website title.
6. a. A works cited entry for an interview begins with the name of the person interviewed, not the person who conducted the interview.
7. b. Elements following the title are separated by commas, and "Narrated by" is spelled out.
8. a. The translator's name is given after the title of the work.
9. a. The access date is not given because the website has an update date.
10. b. A work from a website includes the URL for the work.

Exercise 17-h, page 163

1. False. A URL is never used in an in-text citation.
2. True. The alphabetical organization helps readers quickly find the source that has been cited in the text.
3. False. A list of works cited must give complete publication information for any sources cited in the paper. In-text citations alone are not sufficient.
4. True. MLA provides an option for placement of the author's name: it can appear in a signal phrase or in parentheses.
5. False. When a work's author is unknown, the work is listed under its title.
6. False. In the works cited list, only the first author's name is given in reverse order (last name first). A second author's name is given in normal order (first name first).
7. True. If the author is named in a signal phrase, it is possible that nothing will appear in parentheses.
8. False. MLA style does not use any abbreviation before the page number in an in-text citation.
9. True. Because more than one work will appear in the works cited list, the title is necessary for identifying the exact work that has been cited. The author's name is not enough.
10. True. When a permalink or a DOI is available, use it in the works cited list.

Exercise 18-a, page 165

1. Student A is committing plagiarism. All borrowed language must be in quotation marks.

2. Student B is not committing plagiarism. The writer is seeking advice about how to organize her essay but not using anyone's ideas or language without credit.
3. Student C is committing plagiarism. The student is passing off someone else's work as her own.
4. Student D is committing plagiarism. All borrowed language must be in quotation marks.
5. Student E is committing plagiarism. Writers must cite all sources that they quote from, paraphrase, or summarize.

Exercise 18-b, page 167

Answers will vary.

Exercise 19-a, page 169

Answers will vary.

Exercise 19-b, page 171

Answers will vary.

Exercise 19-c, page 173

1. a; b uses exact language from the source without putting that language in quotation marks.
2. a; b uses sentence structure that is too close to the structure used in the original passage.

Bonus: If the author's name is mentioned in a signal phrase within the sentence, there is no need to repeat the author's name in the parentheses.

Exercise 20-a, page 175 *Suggested revisions:*

1. Active
2. Although these people deserved praise, their open talk endangered escaping slaves.
3. Active
4. Professional slave hunters often caught escaping slaves at the houses of those who talked openly.
5. Any information that increased slave owners' knowledge threatened all slaves.
6. Whenever slave owners suspected some of the escape routes, the slaves lost their courage.
7. Active
8. Active
9. Active

10. Years later, those scars convinced north-
    erners that Douglass spoke the truth about
    slavery.

Exercise 20-b, page 177   *Suggested revision:*

Frederick Douglass changed some of his
ideas about the North after his successful
escape from slavery. Before that time, Douglass
assumed that northerners lacked both money
and culture. In the South, only poor people
owned no slaves. Also, poor people owned no
lovely homes, no pianos, no art, and often no
books. When he first saw New Bedford, Massachusetts, Douglass doubted his own eyesight.
He saw no dilapidated houses or naked children
or barefoot women in New Bedford. Instead, the
beautiful homes with equally beautiful furniture and gardens indicated considerable wealth.
Laborers handled quality merchandise on the
wharves and purchased it in the stores. When
he saw all of this, Douglass happily changed his
ideas about the North.

Exercise 21-a, page 179

1. c;   2. a;   3. a;   4. c;   5. a

Exercise 21-b, page 181   *Suggested revision:*

Leonardo da Vinci's vision of life as one borderless unity affected both his personal life and
his artistic work.

Leonardo did not simply look at the world;
he studied it carefully. Watching the wind ripple
the water in a pond, he was observant, intent,
and serious. Leonardo saw no boundaries in
nature; to him, people and animals were parts
of one creation. He ate no meat because he did
not want to bring death to a fellow creature;
he bought caged songbirds so that he could
set them free. Having no family of his own,
he adopted a boy from another family to be
both his son and his heir. Even right- and left-
handedness were the same to him. He filled his
notebooks with mirror writing, but he wrote
letters, reports, and proposals in the usual way.
When his right hand became crippled, he used
his left.

Leonardo's view of all of life as one creation
led him to artistic innovations. Before Leonardo,
artists had always used outlines to separate
a painting's subject from its background.
Because Leonardo saw everything in nature
as interrelated, he decided that using shadow

and gradation of light and color was better
than using an outline. He wanted one thing to
flow into another the way smoke flows into
air. Looking at Mona Lisa's hand, for instance,
viewers can find no line where one finger ends
and the next one begins; the separation is done
totally with shadows. This unified vision of the
world affected the content of his paintings as
well as the technique. Background and subject
often echo each other in a picture: The drapery
and folds of the subject's clothing may reflect
background scenes of curving vines or rocky
hills or flowing water.

Leonardo recognized the great diversity
surrounding him, but he believed that an even
greater unity supported the diversity and that
his own work was an expression of that unity.

Exercise 22-a, page 183

1. b;   2. b;   3. a;   4. b;   5. a

Exercise 22-b, page 185   *Suggested revision:*

Karl Marx wrote *The Communist Manifesto*, his
most famous work, in collaboration with Friedrich Engels just before the German revolution of
1848. The book has three sections with distinct
characteristics.

In the first section, Marx tries to define terms
accurately and to state his basic assumptions.
He traces the class systems of earlier times and
concludes that there are only two classes in his
day, the bourgeoisie and the proletariat. The
bourgeoisie are the property-owning capitalists; the proletariat are the working class. Marx
asserts that as the bourgeoisie increase their
economic power, they work toward their own
eventual downfall.

Set up in question-and-answer format, the
second section of Marx's *Communist Manifesto*
resembles a debate with a bourgeois sympathizer. Of course, Marx sees only one side of the
debate as being correct. After "defeating" his
opponent on major questions, Marx presents
his own ten-point program in clear, easy-to-
understand, persuasive language.

After developing the second section in detail,
Marx moves on to the *Manifesto*'s final section.
He shows how Communists and other reform
groups work toward the same goals. Reminding workers that they "have nothing to lose
but their chains," Marx calls on them to work
together zealously and actively. In ringing tones,

Marx utters the slogan that can still be heard today: "Workers of the world, unite!"

Exercise 23-a, page 187   *Suggested revisions:*

1. a. Because King didn't have much to write on in the jail, he started writing in the margins of the newspaper in which the article appeared.
   b. Not having much to write on in the jail, King started writing in the margins of the newspaper in which the article appeared.
2. a. Wanting to help King, a black trusty was able to get some scraps of paper for him after a while.
   b. After a while, a black trusty who wanted to help King was able to get some scraps of paper for him.
3. a. After his attorneys were able to give him a pad of paper, King, fired up by the newspaper article, quickly filled the pad.
   b. His attorneys were later allowed to give him a pad of paper. Fired up by the newspaper article, King quickly filled the pad.
4. a. Choosing to write his response to the newspaper article in letter form, King seemed like the biblical Paul to some people.
   b. Because King chose to write his response to the newspaper article in letter form, he seemed like the biblical Paul to some people.
5. a. How were King and Paul alike? A preacher of the Christian faith, like King, Paul wrote some of his famous letters from a prison cell.
   b. How were King and Paul alike? Like King, Paul was a preacher of the Christian faith who wrote some of his famous letters from a prison cell.

Exercise 23-b, page 189   *Suggested revision:*

Everyone has heard of Martin Luther King Jr. After studying for the ministry at Boston University and earning a doctorate in theology, he went home to the South to work as a minister. He started working in civil rights and became the most influential leader of that cause in America. When he died, the victim of an assassin's bullet, his name was almost synonymous with "civil rights." Historians and biographers have recorded his leadership in the fight to gain basic civil rights for all Americans. Many people who know of his civil rights work, however, are not aware of his skill as a writer. In addition to his carefully crafted and emotional speeches, King produced other important writing.

Among King's most famous writings is his "Letter from Birmingham Jail." Written to answer a statement published by eight Alabama ministers that King's work was "unwise and untimely," the letter shows King to be a man who had great patience with his critics. Eager to get these ministers to accept his point of view, King reminds them that they are ministers. Their goodwill, he says, should help them see that his views hold value. Instead of attacking them personally, he analyzes their arguments and then presents his own views. Does he use many of the emotional appeals for which he is justly famous? No, in this letter King depends on logic and reasoning as the tools to win his argument.

Exercise 24-a, page 191

1. a. OK; b. frag
2. a. OK; b. frag
3. a. frag; b. OK
4. a. frag; b. OK
5. a. frag; b. OK

Exercise 24-b, page 193   *Suggested revision:*

Four young Englishmen added a word to the world's vocabulary in the 1960s, a word that became synonymous with the 1960s, especially with the music of that time. That word was, of course, "Beatles." The Beatles became the most famous popular musical group of the twentieth century and have held the loyalty of many fans into the present century.

The Beatles were popular in Liverpool, England, and in Hamburg, Germany, before they came to America on tour and became world famous. Liverpool and Hamburg loved the four young men and their music. The Beatles' favorite club was the Cavern in Liverpool, where they hung out together, played day and night, and attracted many fans. A Liverpool disc jockey first called attention to them, and a Liverpool music critic and record store owner became their first manager. The disc jockey called them "fantastic," saying that they had "resurrected original rock 'n' roll." The music critic who became their manager, Brian Epstein, made them shape up as a group. Promoting them, arranging club dates for them, and badgering record companies for them, he was determined to win a recording contract for this exciting new group.

In England, the record buying led to the publicity. In America, the publicity led to the record buying. Everyone wanted copies of the original singles: "Love Me Do," "Please Please Me," and "From Me to You." In America, audiences made so much noise that no one could hear the music. Crowds of screaming teenagers surrounded the Beatles wherever they went, determined to touch one or more of these famous music makers. Reporters observing the conduct of fans at Beatles' concerts found that they had to invent a new word to describe the wild, almost insane behavior of the fans. They called it "Beatlemania."

Exercise 25-a, page 195 *Suggested revisions:*

1. a. Ralph Chaplin, the only person who wrote anything about Joe Hill before Hill's execution, jotted down just a few notes based on an interview with a drunken sailor.
   b. OK
2. a. OK
   b. Did the state hide evidence? It certainly seemed that way.
3. a. One Wobbly told the police that he had been with Joe Hill in another location on the night of the murder; he also told a detective he could prove Hill's innocence.
   b. OK
4. a. OK
   b. Hill's own attorneys did not do much to help him; their attitude was as negative as that of the prosecutors.
5. a. OK
   b. "I have three prosecutors here. I intend to get rid of two of them," he said.
6. a. OK
   b. How did Hill get that bullet wound in his chest? He told the doctor he had gotten it in a fight over a woman.
7. a. The doctor who treated Hill was not asked to testify about medical aspects of the case. As a matter of fact, his testimony probably would have prevented Hill's conviction.
   b. OK
8. a. OK
   b. The Swedish consul pleaded for him, and President Wilson sent telegrams to the governor of Utah.
9. a. Legend has it that Hill's last words before the firing squad were "Don't mourn for me; organize." In fact, he said, "Yes, aim! Let her go! Fire!"
   b. OK
10. a. Glazer was not the composer of "Joe Hill"; its composers were Earl Robinson and Alfred Hayes.
    b. OK

Exercise 25-b, page 197 *Suggested revision:*

Although he never calls them by name, John Steinbeck immortalizes the Wobblies in *The Grapes of Wrath*. The novel is about the life of the Joad family. Because the Joads have lost their farm during the Depression, the family has come to California seeking work. There is no permanent work for anyone; moreover, the money earned by picking crops is not enough to feed the family.

Union organizers have talked to the workers about organizing and striking. Tom, the oldest Joad son, has listened to them, but he has not yet joined them. Tom is in hiding because he has accidentally killed a man in a fight. He spends all his daylight hours alone, so he has lots of time to think about his family's situation. When Tom becomes convinced that life is unfair for his people, he decides to leave the family, find the union men, and work with them.

Tom is inarticulate when he tries to explain to Ma what he hopes to do. He gropes for words to express his frustration and his hope. Ma asks him how she will know about him, for she worries that he might get killed and she would not know. Tom's reassurances are almost mystical: "Wherever they's a fight so hungry people can eat, I'll be there. . . . An' when our folks eat the stuff they raise an' live in the houses they build—why, I'll be there."

If Tom had had a copy of the Wobblies' "little red song book," he could have found less mystical words. Every copy of the book contained the Wobblies' Preamble, the first sentence of which was unmistakably clear: "The working class and the employing class have nothing in common." Tom would have understood those words; he would have believed them, too.

Exercise 26-a, page 199

1. tells, tries
2. is, is

3. is, leaps
4. is watching, takes
5. tries, are
6. fears, is going
7. have suffered, claims
8. says, are
9. knows, does not believe
10. pretend, cannot get

Exercise 26-b, page 201

comes, tries, are, is, reports, suggests, show, are, wish, are, have

Exercise 27-a, page 203   *Suggested revisions:*

1. When Mother Jones started working in the textile mills at the turn of the twentieth century, she saw "the little gray ghosts," the child laborers who worked from sunup to sundown.
2. OK
3. Mother Jones once led a delegation of three hundred children from Philadelphia to New York to dramatize their plight; some of the newspapers called her "the greatest female agitator in the country."
4. OK
5. When Mother Jones asked for permission to bring three of the children to meet with President Theodore Roosevelt in New York, she was refused. This refusal saddened her because she had hoped for the president's help.
6. Mother Jones asked again and was again refused. This second refusal saddened her even more, but she still did not consider the trip a failure.
7. She told the children and their parents that the children had been successful.
8. OK
9. Thousands of people had learned about the children's plight, and that knowledge was bound to affect their thinking about child labor laws.
10. OK

Exercise 27-b, page 205   *Suggested revision:*

Coal miners' struggles turned into actual war in the Kanawha Valley of West Virginia, where miners were striking. The mine owners dominated the courts and the newspapers; they did not need to worry about the law or public opinion. Although the miners did not want to accept the owners' power, they were often forced to face it. Guards used violent tactics to maintain the mine owners' control, once spraying strikers' tent colonies with machine-gun fire and kicking a pregnant woman so hard that her unborn child died in the womb.

Mary "Mother" Jones urged the miners to fight while she tried to gain the ear of the governor, federal lawmakers, and the public. Records of the fight say that two thousand miners came from outside the valley to help in the battle. The state militia was called in, but the owners got control of the militia soon after it arrived. En route to the state legislature to ask for help, Mother Jones was kidnapped by soldiers, held incommunicado, put in solitary confinement, and tried by a military court. When the new governor of West Virginia, Henry D. Hatfield, investigated, he found a soldier guarding an eighty-year-old pneumonia-ridden woman who had a 104-degree fever.

Word about the Kanawha situation got out, but Governor Hatfield acted first. Out of his work came the Hatfield Agreement. This document, which historians of the labor movement consider a major advance for workers in the United States, forced the companies to recognize the union and to shorten the workday. Even more important, it stipulated that companies must pay wages in US currency. Governor Hatfield also guaranteed civilians the right to civil, not military, trials and dismissed all sentences the military court had imposed—including the twenty-year prison term it had set for Mother Jones.

Exercise 28-a, page 207

1. OK
2. Once when she was traveling with Fred Mooney in Mexico, a crowd stopped the train and urged Mooney and her to open the train window.
3. Mooney and she were not sure whether they should open the window, but they decided to do so. When they did, she and he both were showered with red carnations and blue violets.
4. OK
5. OK
6. When Mooney fretted about her health, it was she who laughed and proposed that they get on with their sightseeing.

7. No one was more excited than she about the idea of a Pan-American Federation of Labor, an organization that would unite workers from Canada to South America.

8. The president of Mexico was as pleased as she at the idea of bringing together all the working people in the hemisphere.

9. OK

10. It was a day Mother Jones long remembered; years later it brought happy smiles to her and her friends whenever they saw carnations and violets or thought of that day's events.

Exercise 28-b, page 209

Though she and a friend would occasionally work together on the friend's campaign, Mother Jones avoided politics most of the time. She, the agitator, had no more interest in politics and political science than she, the labor organizer, had in economic theory. Mother Jones understood one kind of economics, the kind that dealt with wages, benefits, and the cost of bread and housing. The here-and-now problems of the poor called to Mother Jones so strongly that she had to do what she could to stop the injustice she saw around her.

Surprisingly, Mother Jones was not a supporter of women's suffrage. When the fight to win women's right to vote came along, it was not she who supported it. She and her people were the working classes, both men and women, and neither she nor they had much patience for the "society women" who led the movement. As far as Mother Jones was concerned, well-dressed women parading down the city streets carrying placards and banners did not help working men and women obtain a decent life. Mother Jones objected to their spending time and energy and money on activities that would not help her kind of people. Nor was she interested in helping a cause that would benefit only women; her concern was for all workers, regardless of gender. She seemed not to understand that the votes of the miners' wives might do as much to help the working men as her agitating and organizing did.

Exercise 29-a, page 211

Women who led the suffrage movement never used violence, but they thought of themselves as waging a war. They tried different strategies in different places and coordinated their various attacks. Some concentrated on state and local voting rights for women; others worked for national suffrage. In Washington, DC, they picketed, demonstrated, and built and maintained "perpetual watchfires" in which they burned the speeches on democracy that President Wilson was giving in Europe.

When the protesters were arrested at the White House in 1917, police had to use their personal cars to carry the many prisoners they arrested. After the women and some of their supporters were tried and found guilty, the judge got so tired of sentencing them that when he reached twenty-six, he dismissed all the others.

The women's organizing and demonstrating finally paid off. On May 21, 1919, the House of Representatives passed the Nineteenth Amendment, giving women the right to vote, and sent it to the Senate. On June 4, the Senate approved it and passed it along to the states for ratification.

Women's groups kept up the pressure on the states during the long, tense ratification process. When, after more than a year, thirty-five states had ratified the amendment, it all came down to one man's vote in Tennessee. Whom does history remember as the hero of ratification? It was a young legislator named Harry Burn, who cast the tie-breaking vote. On August 24, the governor of Tennessee certified the vote and sent the results to Washington.

The US Secretary of State had told his staff to wake him as soon as the certificate arrived. He wanted to avoid a formal signing in the presence of the campaigning women. Nevertheless, on August 26, 1920, more than seventy years after women had first begun to organize for suffrage, it was now official: Women in the United States had the right to vote.

Exercise 29-b, page 213

Many historians have agreed that the women's suffrage movement in the United States is rooted in the Seneca Falls Convention of 1848. The convention was organized by Elizabeth Cady Stanton and Lucretia Mott, after Mott was denied a seat as a delegate at an antislavery convention in London.

The Seneca Falls Convention is best known for a document produced by Stanton called the Declaration of Sentiments. Stanton's declaration remains one of the most important documents in American women's history. Modeled on the Declaration of Independence (1776), the Declaration of Sentiments lists eighteen grievances—but these are grievances of women against their treatment by men and male-dominated society. Stanton's declaration explicitly states that "all men and women are created equal" and that women "demand the equal station to which they are entitled."

A modern reader doesn't have to read more than a few sentences of each document to see the similarities between the two. In fact, it has been said that the Declaration of Sentiments might have been rejected if its format hadn't seemed so familiar to those who attended the convention. The Declaration of Independence demands that men in America, like men in England, be represented in government. The Declaration of Sentiments argues that women, like men, should be represented in government. The women's document goes so far as to suggest that American women should have the right to vote. In 1848, this idea was shocking—so shocking that it would take seventy-two years for women's right to vote to become a reality.

Exercise 29-c, page 214

1. Eighty percent of the immigrants who migrated to the United States in the 1980s were Asian or Latin American.
2. The number of Asians who were living in the United States more than doubled between 1970 and 1980.
3. People from the Philippines, China, and Korea have been regular immigrants to the United States.
4. Since 1975, a rush of immigrant refugees has been arriving in the United States.
5. In less than a seven-year period, 600,000 refugees from Vietnam, Laos, and Cambodia came to the United States.

Exercise 30-a, page 215

1. The animals loved to watch her dance; her tiny feet seemed never to touch the path.
2. OK
3. Rhodopis's shoes had leather soles, but the toes had gold on them.
4. When Rhodopis danced, the shoes sparkled; they seemed alive.

5. Jealous, the servant girls gave her more chores; by nighttime, Rhodopis was almost too tired for a single dance.
6. Pharaoh, the ruler of Egypt, sent out an invitation for all his subjects to appear at a court festival.
7. Everyone wanted to go to the festival; Rhodopis looked forward to dancing there.
8. OK
9. While Rhodopis was doing the laundry, a hippopotamus splashed into the water.
10. OK

Exercise 30-b, page 216 *Suggested revision:*

People all over the world have stories that are part of their culture. Many cultures have a creation story that explains how the world came to be. Sometimes the story tells how a single piece of the world got its characteristics. It is not surprising that these stories exist; what is surprising is how similar the stories are. Consider the Cinderella story, for example. Cinderella has different names in different places, and details of her adventure are not the same; but the basic story echoes around the world.

In Egypt, she is called Rhodopis (the word means "rosy cheeked"). Rhodopis is a Greek slave in an Egyptian home. She does not have eyes or hair like anyone else in the home. Her green eyes look quite different from the eyes of the other girls. Their dark, straight hair almost never gets tangled; her yellow, curly hair blows into a tangled mass around her face. Her light-skinned face turns red and burns when she is in the sun too long. When someone calls her "Rosy Rhodopis," she blushes, and her cheeks become rosier.

Unable to make friends with the other girls, Rhodopis turns to the animals in the nearby woods and streams for companionship.

Exercise 31-a, page 217

1. One of the earliest contributors to the young adult dystopian genre is Lois Lowry, whose novel *The Giver* won the Newbery Medal in 1994.
2. *The Giver* is still taught in schools alongside the older dystopian novels *Brave New World* and *Animal Farm*.
3. OK
4. Parents of adolescents at the time thumbed through *The Giver* with trepidation, a feeling

with which many readers approached the book.

5. OK

6. Jonas, the protagonist, is given the role of receiver of memories.

7. As Jonas accepts memories from the current receiver, a wise old man known as the Giver, Jonas experiences love, loss, color, the sun, snow, terror, and excitement for the first time.

8. When the Giver tells Jonas the true meaning of the ceremony known as "release," the two decide to join forces to save their community.

9. To give the memories of the past back to the community, Jonas must escape to Elsewhere and leave the Giver behind to help people cope with the flood of emotion and changes to come.

10. Although subject matter such as this can be challenging for young readers, Lowry has said, "Pretending that there are no choices to be made — reading only books, for example, which are cheery and safe and nice — is a prescription for disaster for the young."

Exercise 31-b, page 219

1. a. Their audacity, which we see in Katniss in *The Hunger Games*, reflects the individuality and self-assertion portrayed in more and more young female protagonists.
b. Correct

2. a. Dystopian works tend to be less angst-filled and romanticized than other young adult works like the Twilight series.
b. Correct

3. a. Scott Westerfeld's Uglies series imagines a postapocalyptic world in which all teenagers are ugly until radical surgery at age sixteen makes them into supermodel "pretties."
b. Correct

4. a. Correct
b. The fact that *Uglies* and the books that followed it were wildly popular proves that girls and young women want to read about challenging topics that they can relate to.

5. a. Correct
b. The dystopian novel, like its science fiction counterpart, has the power to examine and change the way our society functions.

Exercise 31-c, page 221

Young adult dystopian literature is a popular genre with a growing fan base worldwide; its books are characterized by degradation, totalitarian states, and dehumanization. With the release of the film version of Suzanne Collins's *The Hunger Games*, the genre has amassed a following similar to that of wizards and vampires in fiction and pop culture. Writers such as Lois Lowry and M. T. Anderson have been producing award-winning dystopian work for years. But the wild popularity of such writers reveals that young readers welcome the serious, dark work being marketed to them. The dystopian novel takes risks, and teenagers like risks. In sophisticated ways that are satisfying to young readers, these books depict pain, loss, and the anxieties of growing up.

Dystopia is the opposite of utopia, which is any system of political or social perfection, an ideal place or state. Dystopia signifies regression. It is a fictional society characterized by poverty, oppression, disease, or overcrowding. The world in a dystopian novel is recognizable as a warped version of our own; people may survive an epic tragedy, often environmental or political, and survivors form a society that curtails freedoms to protect citizens. A hero or heroine must triumph over terrible odds to better the society and restore harmony. The novels are often violent. While the violence may disturb parents, teenagers want stories with weight and intensity. They want to immerse themselves in a world where there is no happy ending, a world that challenges and shocks them and where they can see the best and the worst of humanity.

Exercise 32-a, page 223

1. Deborah Sampson never dreamed that she would someday fight in battles for American independence, much less that the battles' outcomes might depend on her.

2. Because her parents' income was not enough to support their children, her parents sent Deborah to live with relatives in another town.

3. Later she was sent to live in a foster family with ten sons; the sons' acceptance of her was wholehearted, and one son became her fiancé when she grew up.

4. The Revolutionary War wasn't over when news of his death reached Deborah; she wasn't long in making a decision.
5. Determined that his place should become hers, she enlisted under a man's name.

Exercise 32-b, page 224

1. OK
2. It's clear that Deborah Sampson thought so; she enlisted twice to fight for hers.
3. OK
4. Though drinking was not a habit of hers, she spent her first evening as a soldier copying other new soldiers' behavior.
5. Coming to the aid of this very noisy, very drunk, and very sick "buddy" of theirs, they soon were asking, "Who's this?"

Exercise 32-c, page 225

During the 1990 troubles in Panama, American television and newspaper reporters had an exciting piece of news. They reported that for the first time American female soldiers had been engaged in actual combat. Acting as her soldiers' leader, Captain Linda Bray led her troops into combat. Names of two additional women who were involved in combat, Staff Sergeant April Hanley and Private First Class Christina Proctor, were reported in the newspapers. Theirs were the only names reported, although other women also took part in the fighting.

It wasn't the first time an American woman had fought in an American battle, but it's not likely that many people are aware of that fact. The Civil War had its female fighters too. Loreta Janeta Velazquez fought for the Confederates in the Civil War after her husband's death. Like many other women whose husbands were killed in that war, she must have asked herself, "Who's going to take his place in battle?" The decision to fight was hers alone. Someone is sure to ask how that was possible, especially in those days. Military identification was not very sophisticated in the 1860s. Someone's willingness to fight was that person's major qualification, and each fighting unit needed to replace its losses as fast as possible. Velazquez simply disguised herself in men's clothing, found a troop needing replacements, and joined the fight. Loreta Janeta Velazquez was Linda Bray's Civil War predecessor.

Exercise 33-a, page 227

1. The doctor answered, "You can do nothing but pray."
2. When the bandages were removed and the shades were opened to let in the bright sunlight, the doctor asked, "What do you see?"
3. "Nothing," said the boy. "I see nothing."
4. The village priest said, "I have recently seen a remarkable school." He had just returned from a trip to Paris.
5. "In this school," he added, "blind students are taught to read."
6. "You didn't say 'read,' did you?" asked the boy's father.
7. The boy responded to the priest's words as if they were a trick of some kind: "Now you are joking with me. How can such a thing be possible?"
8. The boy, Louis, thought it would be great fun to visit that school someday.
9. His father promised, "We will go soon, Louis."
10. And so it happened that ten-year-old Louis Braille entered the National Institute for Blind Youth and began the long effort to erase the fear people had of even the word "blind." [Or the word *blind* can be italicized, without quotation marks.]

Exercise 33-b, page 229

Louis Braille entered the National Institute for Blind Youth in Paris when he was ten. At twelve, he was already experimenting with a system of raised dots on paper known as "night-writing," which was used by the military. Institute teachers decided that night-writing was impractical, but Louis became proficient at it. When Charles Barbier, inventor of the system, visited the institute, Louis told him, "Your symbols are too large and too complicated." Impressed, Barbier encouraged him and said that since Louis was blind himself, he might discover the magic key that had eluded his teachers.

Louis Braille wanted a system that could transcribe everything from a textbook on science to a poem like Heinrich Heine's "Loreley." At fifteen, he had worked out his own system of six dots arranged in various patterns. "Read to me," he said to one of his teachers, "and I will take down your words." As the teacher read, Louis punched dots onto his paper and then read the passage back without error. The teacher exclaimed, "Remarkable!" Government officials, not impressed enough to take any action, said simply that Braille should be encouraged. "You didn't say 'encouraged,' did you?" asked Braille. He wanted official acceptance, not simply encouragement. "The system has proved itself," said Louis. "We have been using it for five years now."

For most people, the word "Braille" [or *Braille*] itself now means simply a system of reading and writing used by blind people; for blind people, it means freedom and independence. Braille himself died before his system was recognized beyond the institute. The plaque on the house of his birth, however, records the world's recognition of his work with these words: "He opened the doors of knowledge to all those who cannot see."